The Bipolar Advantage

Tom Wootton

Bipolar Advantage
www.BipolarAdvantage.com

Cover design by Don Farnsworth

ISBN 0-9774423-0-6

Table of Contents

Part 2: A Successful Bipolar Lifestyle

"This is Bullshit"

"This is bullshit. There is nothing good about being bipolar." I had just finished putting together the list of good things about bipolar with my first ever Bipolar In Order Workshop, when John angrily got up from his chair and walked out. I had carefully planned the seminar and its success hinged on getting agreement from the audience that there are some good things about bipolar if we could just see them. There was such great participation that the list of the good things was just as long as the list of bad things we had previously put together. I tried to make a passionate argument for my cause, but the wind had been taken out of my sails and all I could do was break for lunch.

It's not as though I was new at giving seminars. I was very successful teaching accelerated learning techniques to teachers, professors, and corporate trainers. I had been a highly paid technology trainer and my client list was Fortune 500 companies across many industry segments. I THOUGHT I had seen it all. I was well prepared.

Even though this was a new workshop, I had taught most of the segments before. The teaching techniques were so familiar I could do them in my sleep. I had no idea that this was only the beginning of the hardest, yet most rewarding project of my life. I thought I knew how to handle a tough audience. Boy, was I in for a surprise. How could I have been so unprepared for a whole group of people just like me?

I quit my high stress dot com career in July of 2000. I had $2.5 million in stock and was set for life. I was exhausted from four years of world travel and was looking forward to a great life ahead. My wife Ellen and I lived in our dream house in Mill Valley, California. I was looking forward to driving my offshore race boat in San Francisco Bay and enjoying life.

The four years before I left my job were the hardest of my life. I was making so much money I couldn't quit, but I was miserable and hated what I had become. My reputation at my company was mercurial at best. I often went into rages and threatened to 'go postal' and blow up the office. I went into screaming tantrums for no reason at all, often just after receiving a compliment for a job well done. I regularly yelled at my wife, Ellen, that she didn't understand how hard it was for me to make it all happen.

Up until then my record for staying at the same job was 9 months. Four years at the same job almost killed me. I waited for the four year anniversary so I could collect the final allotment of stock and quit on the very day it was issued. For good measure I sued the bastards on my way out.

Why didn't anybody see that I was mentally unstable? Years earlier a doctor friend thought it was funny that he had never met a person who was manic all the time. Why didn't he tell me what that meant?

Two months after I left my job the stock market crashed. I was in the middle (so I thought) of a down period and incapable of making a decision. I sat and watched as my stocks lost over $300,000 a month in value. I couldn't think clearly enough to sell. Eventually I had to sell my house and move to San Diego where I could buy a house for practically nothing compared to the San Francisco Bay Area.

I was broke, depressed, and had nothing to live for. I didn't get out of bed for months. Finally, out of desperation, I took a job as a car salesman at a Cadillac dealership because I had never done that before. I thought that if those idiots can do it, so can I!

Why didn't anyone notice? I slept under my desk at work every day. I started conflicts with fellow workers by accusing them of plotting behind my back. I acted more than just a little bizarre, but since I fixed the computers around the place they tolerated me just like others always have.

I went to the doctor regularly, complaining of back pain, stomach problems, headaches, etc. Finally the clinic told me that I needed a regular doctor instead of just dropping in. When I met my new doctor for the first visit he said, "Did you ever consider you might be depressed?" "Not me, I'm the happiest guy I ever met," I replied. "Besides, I am just under a lot of stress. I lost $2.5 million, had to move from my dream home, and am recovering from a very stressful career."

For the first time in my life someone didn't let me get away with it. "Do you know the difference between stress and depression?" "No." "Stress is the result of the things that happen to you. Depression is your inability to deal with the stress and makes you unable to function normally. The reason you keep having physical problems is because you are depressed." This turned out to be one of the moments that changed my life forever.

The doctor talked me into taking Lexapro against my strongest arguments. He used the 'you'll only have to take it temporarily until you get back on your feet' argument. The argument worked, the Lexapro didn't. He switched my prescription to Effexor and it seemed to be working better. When my wife's insurance ended and mine began, I had to switch doctors right when I finally found one that could help me. (Isn't America's health care system great? I had to change to another health plan just a week after I started to take Effexor.)

Effexor was the worst nightmare of my life. I started hallucinating, became paranoid, and was downright uncontrollable. My boss finally had to fire me. My new doctor didn't know anything, of course, and sent me to the psychiatric department. I had to wait forever for an appointment.(But don't we have the best health care in the world?)

I got to the second floor and the elevator opened. To the right was the Optometry Department and to the left - Psychiatry. (Does everyone feel like somebody is going to know you are crazy if they see you there? To this day I still have the same feeling, but I like it now.) Anyway, I sat down, filled out the questionnaire, and waited to be called.

When I sat down with my counselor she took one look at the form and said, "You are not depressed, you have bipolar disorder" like that was some kind of great news.

Once she explained what that meant I had to agree, and in a peculiar sort of way, it IS great news. For the first time in my life I started to understand why I had done everything - and I mean EVERYTHING. It was like the 'unifying theory of all life for Tom'! I went home and started on the most incredible journey of my life. (Did I mention that it has also been the most painful?)

I read everything I could find about bipolar. I had regular sessions with Roberta, my counselor. Thank God Roberta has an hour each visit because I need to talk about this and work this out. I had rare sessions with my shrink. (Actual doctors of Psychiatry don't have time for anything but pushing pills. Five minutes with him and I walk out with a prescription.)

The trouble with all the information I was getting was that there did not seem to be much hope.

Bipolar is a curse worse than death. Not only do up to 40% of us attempt to end it with suicide[1], half succeed. It ranks right up there with the all time killers, and in certain age groups bipolar IS the number one killer. What makes it worse than death is how horrible life can be on the way. If you haven't been there yourself, you have no idea what it is like. Too bad most of the so called 'experts' have not been there, because they are the ones telling us how to handle it.

Roberta kept telling me that there was hope, and I finally said, "Show me." She sent me to a bipolar support group made up of actual victims.

---

1 www.psychlaws.org/BriefingPapers/BP6.pdf

There is no doubt in my mind that my first visit to a support group was one of the worst experiences imaginable. I don't know how I could have been so naive. I was expecting those people to give me hope. I thought they were going to tell me how they have learned to handle being bipolar, and that they are now living productive and happy lives. (If they were living happy lives, why were they in a support group?)

The meeting was in a local mental hospital. I went into the room and everyone was sitting around a big dining room table. There were about fifteen people, including Ellen and myself. Michael, the group leader, welcomed us and outlined the guidelines: everybody gets a chance to talk, you don't have to talk unless you want to, after each speaker the others may comment if the speaker says it's OK, nothing said in the room leaves the room, none of us are doctors, etc.

The first person started with "I am so depressed I am thinking of killing myself. I have tried every drug for twelve years and none of them are working..." She looked awful. Everybody said something about feeling sorry for her and we went on to the next person. I was stunned, but looking forward to the next one. He started out with "I know how you feel. I am checked in here because I attempted to kill myself last night. It has been fifteen years and..."

By now I was in shock. I started shaking inside and it was all I could do to hold back the tears. The next person started in the same vein and now I was just plain FREAKING OUT. Michael finally noticed and asked if I was OK. "No I am not OK. I came here to get some hope and now I have no hope at all." Everybody jumped in and calmed me down with reassurances. I'll always remember Becca. She took charge and handled it like a pro. They all agreed that I needed to check in right away since they had seen it all before and I was obviously in big trouble.

I didn't want to check myself into a nut house. "These people are whacko. I am not going to get locked in here. They will give me shock treatments and I'll end up like the guy in 'One Flew Over The Cuckoo's Nest.'" I didn't say any of that out loud, of course, but I calmed down and assured them that I was going to be just fine.

Poor Ellen. Poor me! If we hadn't lived a half hour from town, she would have taken me to the emergency room right away. We got into the house and Ellen went to check on our new kittens. Within minutes, I was screaming that she loved the kittens more than me and went into an unbelievable tirade that lasted five minutes. I was so out of control it was unbelievable. Wait a minute. Who was I kidding? I had done this all my life. But now I was feeling guilty about it for the first time. The guilty feeling sent me in the opposite direction. Ellen followed me into the bedroom where I lay in bed shaking and crying. It was so bad I couldn't even breathe. I was sure I was going to die. Five minutes later while I was in the shower trying to calm down, I started screaming again. This went on forever. Five minutes of hell followed by five minutes of the opposite hell.

The next morning I threw out the Effexor and started a month-long fast to clean out my system because I just KNEW the Effexor was causing my rapid cycling. Nobody ever accused me of doing something half-assed. I had fasted many times before and am very familiar with the benefits of both short and long fasts. What shocked everyone at the support group was that my doctor had not prescribed

Lithium (a mood stabilizer) to balance the Effexor. I go back to my shrink and next thing you know I am fairly stable and on lithium.

Roberta sent me to a nurse-led six week workshop that was run so badly I walked out the second night and wrote a complaint to the hospital. Of course they wouldn't listen to me: I was 'crazy'. I decided what the bipolar world needed was someone who not only understood the disorder, but also knew how to do a seminar. Who better than me?

I told my shrink about my new workshop idea and he replied, "You should leave that to the professionals," meaning those with a Ph.D. who didn't actually have any first-hand experience. I decided that he was full of shit and set out to put together my own seminar that was going to give people hope.

I designed a great course. It was carefully crafted to bring out the knowledge that every bipolar already knew but had never brought to the surface before. I know how to facilitate a discussion that makes everyone else the expert and me just the guy asking questions and writing their answers down.

I've done this so many times before. All I have to do is start out with everybody calling out all the terrible things about bipolar that they can think of. Then I teach them brainstorming and I can even convince them that bipolars actually have an advantage in that regard. We all have racing thoughts that go in every direction, so that will be an easy sell. Then play a game that will get them in the mood to see the bright side of things about bipolar and I am there. Use the momentum to create a list of all the good things and after lunch I can move on to acceptance and introspection. End the day with conversation about how they have opened their eyes for the first time to the possibility that we can win the war against bipolar. The next day of the workshop will be easy. Just give a bunch of exercises and they can leave with a battle plan and the hope they need to achieve success!

What I wasn't prepared for is that these people are BIPOLAR. Sure, running a seminar is easy when the participants have their job on the line. They might challenge you, but they are not going to step over the line and get themselves fired. It's a whole new ball game with this crowd. Why didn't I plan that at least some of the audience would be like me?

By the time I got over John walking out, I had to contend with worse: grandstanding manics who think that what they have to say is so significant we should listen to them all day, and depressed cases that are too caught in their own pain to pay attention. Both were competing for the prize of undoing my efforts. What a ride!

Never do I survive a workshop without wondering why I do this. And I mean SURVIVE. I am more worn out from these workshops than from anything I have ever done. So why do I do it? Because it is the only thing I have ever done that has such meaning and such great rewards.

By now I was the president of DBSA North County, the local chapter of the Depression and Bipolar Support Alliance[1]. DBSA is a consumer-led organization dedicated to

---

1 www.dbsalliance.org

educating everyone who will listen about a topic that has affected all of us in such a major way.

Which brings me back to John. John's wife Virginia had called me in desperation. Virginia was upset because John had not been out of bed in two years. She was desperate and I was her last hope. I talked her into bringing John to the first Bipolar In Order workshop and assured her that it would help her understand, and help John see some hope.

After John walked out, he took a nap for the rest of the day. Virginia stayed in the class and seemed to enjoy it, although she was visibly worried about John. The next morning Ellen rearranged the chairs so that John had to look at the list of good things instead of the list of bad things that he had been facing yesterday. John stayed most of the day, and although he was argumentative, he participated in all of the exercises and discussions.

It was at the end of the second day that I knew I was on to something. Everybody was talking about how much they liked the course when John piped up. He pointed at the list of good things and said, "I want to be like that." It was the most rewarding moment. I passed out a questionnaire about the seminar and anxiously waited for everyone to leave so I could read the replies.

I think I may have helped change John's life, but he definitely changed mine forever. When asked what one thing he got from the course, his reply was, "I need to take responsibility for my life." His reply to, "What one thing are you going to do first?" was "Get out of bed tomorrow." I was thrilled. The responses from the other participants were great too, but the feedback I got from John went beyond my wildest dreams.

I followed up in a few days and both John and Virginia were overjoyed. John not only got out of bed, he shaved, cleaned up quite nicely and went out and got a job! It has been a few years and four jobs later, but he is still working. Every time I think about what I want to do with my life, I think of John and I know that I have found my calling.

Why Listen to Me?

OK, so I'm bipolar. Big deal. Well, at least I know it from the inside instead of just looking at it from outside. It's like the story I made up for my daughter to illustrate the difference between those who just go to church and those who seek a direct experience of God. You can read the label of the yogurt container and debate the mix of ingredients, nutritional values, etc., but until you open it up and take a bite you don't have a clue.

Tell me you have never taken a thought or an action to such extremes that you could not share it with anyone, and I will call you a liar, or worse - boring. One thing about bipolars, we are definitely not boring. Haven't you ever wondered why you think or do things that you are afraid to tell others about for fear that they will judge you harshly or think you are weird? Bipolar people take everything to the extreme; emotions, thoughts, actions, EVERYTHING. My two mottos ever since I can remember are: "If it's worth doing, it's worth overdoing" and "too much of a good thing is not enough." If you don't think that's weird, it is only because you haven't heard the details of what that means yet.

Don't you sometimes wonder 'why'? Why, for example, was I intimately fascinated with the relationship of my breath to my thoughts and feelings at an age when other boys were just discovering their penis? (Sure, I was discovering mine too, but only fellow bipolars have taken that discovery to a level that would shock even a porn star. I should know; I was a porn star. But enough about sex for now. It is one of the top ten items on the list according the clinical research about bipolar people, so we will be covering sex in a later chapter.) I have been wondering 'why?' my whole life and once I was diagnosed it all started to make sense.

My diagnosis for 'bipolar disorder type I' was perhaps the most significant moment of my life. For me it was a death sentence. The odds are 40% that I will try to kill myself, probably in a very creative way. I am still shocked every time I think that thought, but I am a fool to pretend it can't happen. Meanwhile, I go from ecstatic states to the depths of hell and everything in between. Like I said, bipolars are not boring. On the other hand, having been diagnosed as bipolar helps me to finally understand the 'why?' question.

The months following my diagnosis were awful. The months before were too, so who cares? I now had an answer to the 'why' question. I became fascinated with remembering thoughts and events from my past and checking to see if they really happened. I called my sister, "Did I really freak out and pull a knife on you when I was ten?" "Yep." To my last boss, "Did I really threaten to kill everyone on a regular basis? Did I really sleep under my desk and act like I was from another planet?" "Everybody said you were mercurial, but we had no idea you were bipolar. Yes, you were a maniac, but we just thought you were passionate to the extreme."

The first full blown instance of mania was when I was 9 years old. My father brought home a set of books that allowed me to learn at my own pace. To say I devoured them is an understatement. I stayed up all night for three months and went from the fourth to the 9th grade level in every subject. Unfortunately, I was bored with school ever since and mostly just slept through every class in a strange otherworldly trance. Interestingly, I got an 'A' on every test I ever took anyway. In math, for example, I didn't even do the steps necessary to get the answer. To this day, I have no idea why correct answers always just popped into my head when I knew nothing about the subject.

I wonder about the many times I quit my job for no reason and stayed in bed for three months. How about the times I would work for 9 months at a time without so much as an hour of sleep? Sure enough, every call ended not only in verification, but also in discovery of my self and a deeper relationship with those I talked with. Although a huge part of my focus was always my spiritual life, including two years spent living in a monastery, I never had the insights I was gaining now. And still am.

"Write a book," they always say. Whenever I tell people about even a small part of my life, they say, "you should write a book. Your life is so fascinating." Well, here it is. I won't spill all the beans since that is not the point of this book, but for illustrative purposes this book will be a combination of my experiences and methods for you to come to a greater awareness of your own life.

Some of this is shocking, but I have learned that honesty is the best way to get others to admit to themselves who they really are. I also know from running support groups and workshops that I am not very different from any garden-variety bipolar, so it is not a shock to them. What is shocking is that someone is willing to admit it.

There is also a good chance that this book is not for you. You may be content to just read the label of the yogurt container instead of tasting life. Reality is hard for everyone, especially when confronted by someone unafraid to admit to it. I am not trying to shock or offend anyone, but if you are sincerely interested in finding out what is REALLY going on and dealing with the REAL issues instead of pretending they aren't there; this book is for you.

Why should you listen to me? I'm not a doctor. I don't even play one on TV. I only discovered that I was bipolar in 2002. Hardly a seasoned expert with twenty years of experience. Just because it took the doctors 45 years to figure it out does not mean I was unconscious the whole time.

When I first put together the Bipolar In Order Workshop I told my shrink and his reaction was "you should leave that up to the professionals." "I am a professional," was my reply, but it fell on deaf ears. To him, "professional" means someone who reads the yogurt label, believes that teaching is sharing his vast knowledge, and that the students should just shut up and memorize. We bipolars are experts of our own experience, and I am an expert at bringing it out of people.

I spent my life studying brain and consciousness research, lived in a monastery for 2 years, and could go on for way more than anyone cares to hear. Most importantly, I taught "accelerative learning" to teachers, professors, and corporate trainers for 15 years in various capacities and know that real teaching is not sharing what I know as much as helping the audience to bring out what they already know themselves.

I also know from direct experience that many people tell me things they will not tell their parents, friends, spouse, minister, shrink, or even themselves until I help them to feel comfortable. You see, I have another Bipolar Advantage; I have been there and I want to help. I've found that bipolars are very willing to be honest, once they accept their illness and find support.

So why does that make me qualified to claim that there is such an audacious thing as a Bipolar Advantage? In an odd sort of way, it was a relief to finally have a diagnosis. I had always thought there was something strange about me. Now I know that I'm not just crazy, extreme, bizarre, etc. - I have 'The Bipolar Advantage'! It might sound outrageous right now, but those who have taken the workshop have all agreed that there are definite advantages to being bipolar. Once you read the book or take the workshop I am sure you will agree.

My greatest desire is for this book to bring hope. Hope to those recently diagnosed with bipolar. Hope to those who have been struggling with it for a long time. Hope to those who find themselves in a supportive role with someone that they care about.

Part 1: Knowing Who You Really Are

What Is Bad About Bipolar?

Also Known as Manic - Depression

Affective disorders include both depression and manic depression. Manic depression is often characterized by cycles of manic and depressive behavior. Common symptoms of the manic phase of bipolar disorder or manic-depression include: Heightened mood, exaggerated optimism and self-confidence, Grandiose ideas and delusions, inflated sense of self-importance, Decreased need for sleep without experiencing fatigue, Excessive irritability and/or aggressive behavior, Increased physical and mental activity, Racing speech, flight of ideas, impulsiveness, Poor judgement or reckless behavior such as spending sprees, rash business decisions, or sexual promiscuity. Common symptoms of the depressive phase of bipolar disorder or manic-depression include: Prolonged feelings of sadness, anxiety, or hopelessness, Sense of impending doom or disaster, Reduced enjoyment and pleasure, Loss of energy and motivation, Low self-esteem, feelings of worthlessness or guilt, Indecisiveness, reduced concentration, slow thinking, Significant changes in appetite and/or sleep patterns, Social withdrawal, Recurrent thoughts of death or suicide. Key Facts About Bipolar Disorder According to the National Depressive and Manic-Depressive Association, manic-depression or bipolar disorder affects 2.5 million adult Americans sometime during their lifetime. While people can be afflicted anytime during their lifetime, a typical age of onset for bipolar disorder is in the range of 18 to 22 years. Fifteen to twenty percent of people with untreated bipolar disorder commit suicide.(1)

You can read descriptions of Bipolar until your eyes are sore (tiny text - get it?), but until you hear someone

---

1 www.mddaboston.org/bipolar.html

describe the same things you experience, or feel the acceptance when someone says "me too" for the first time, you don't have a clue. We look deeply into what bipolar is all about by sharing our first-hand experiences. The Bipolar In Order Workshop includes the part that has been left out in all discussions until now - what is GOOD about bipolar. In the process, we learn to confront head-on exactly what bipolar is all about in an environment of support and acceptance. Just like when you try a new brand of yogurt, the label only describes the ingredients; you have to open it up and taste it to know if it is right for you. By sharing with each other in a directed environment, we come to understand bipolar better than we ever did before.

The bad things about bipolar

Make no mistake, bipolar is a fate worse than death. With all the great literature, movies, drama, music and art in the world that tries to portray it, bipolar is still almost totally misunderstood by those who have never experienced it themselves. People suffer incredible pain from accidents, cancer, and other illnesses, but few of them get to the point where they take their own life to make it stop. Some say up to 40% of bipolars do. Bipolar is one of the biggest causes of death[1] in every age group. Because bipolar is so horrible, it really is an audacious claim to say that there is actually a Bipolar Advantage.

Most people diagnosed with bipolar go to the doctor because of depression. Who would go in and say "I am so happy what's wrong with me?" But depression is not the

---

1 http://www.healthyplace.com/communities/bipolar/related/suicide_9.asp

whole picture by any means. Mania can be every bit as bad and it's even worse for those around us. If you think it is bad being with someone who's depressed, just wait till a manic person comes unglued on you. You might even get a taste of depression yourself.

Depression and mania might be the two poles of bipolar, but there is a whole range of other symptoms that give them both a run for their money. Paranoia, delusions and hallucinations, spending sprees (often ending in bankruptcy), sexual promiscuity, excessive irritability, aggressive behavior, impulsiveness, poor judgment, distractibility, prolonged sadness or unexplained crying spells, significant changes in appetite and sleep patterns, irritability, anger, worry, agitation, anxiety, pessimism, indifference, loss of energy, persistent lethargy, feelings of guilt, worthlessness, inability to concentrate, indecisiveness, inability to take pleasure in former interests, social withdrawal, unexplained aches and pains, recurring thoughts of death or suicide, and more are all associated with bipolar. And these are just the ones they ask you about when making the diagnosis. (And did I mention suicide?)

There are so many great books about the horrors of bipolar. It is not my intention to be among them. Besides, listing symptoms and the percent of people who have them will do no good in helping you to relate. You'll start to get the sense for how bad it can get if you to take some LSD, tell everybody who loves you to fuck off, have sex with fifty strangers, kill your dog, break both legs, cut up your arms and legs with razor blades, take something that will make you puke non-stop, and tie yourself to the bed in a dark room for a month. Or maybe just speak out against the government and they will do it for you. (Did I mention paranoia?)

Acknowledging the bad about bipolar is one of the most healing aspects of the Bipolar In Order Workshop. Every time I lead a group through it, we always find out that we share many, if not all, of the same set of horrors. Although there is so much in common with every group, there are always a few new items that have not been mentioned before. The important thing is not to analyze whether the doctors would call it part of bipolar. It is part of our hell and it is healing to get it all out on paper. It is even more healing to meet other people who have similar experiences.

The process of building the list is so amazing. If I haven't convinced everyone that this is a workshop of participation, they sure get it now. I write furiously while people call out symptoms. So often others chime in with agreement that an item is shared. (Can I get an Amen?) Those that have never opened up before become empowered to share. (Can I get another Amen?) Sooner or later someone says it was like a religious experience. (Hallelujah!) It is unbelievable for even the long time veterans of support groups to see it all right there on several sheets of paper. I make sure that nothing is left out and get everyone to agree that this list fully represents the hell that we share.

How can anyone put a list together of the hell of bipolar and get excited? I don't know, it just happens. To finally let it out produces an incredible feeling of release. It feels like a miracle to find others that you KNOW understand. Even the participants who don't have it become excited that they finally have a sense of what bipolar really is. The relief is especially prominent in those without bipolar who have read everything they can, but still somehow feel that they can't relate to the loved ones that are afflicted. It is a major bonding experience for all of us.

In our workshops we have come up with an incredible list of traits that we associate with bipolar. Maybe the researchers will decide that some of them don't belong, but what do we care? These are the things about ourselves that we have to face and accept.

Why even face such a painful realization of our bad traits? We need to face reality and deal with it in the open. You don't have to admit it to anyone else, but you will be amazed when someone helps you to be comfortable enough to at least admit it to yourself. How are we going to get anywhere if we don't even let ourselves know where we are now?

The following traits were called out by the participants of the workshop as bad things they associate with bipolar. These are not the clinical items you find in a textbook. These items are what hurt real patients whether they are associated with bipolar or not.

**loss of control   lost friends   shame
guilt   spending sprees   confusion
no focus   reckless behavior   suicide
bad driving   broken laws
depression   self abuse   insomnia
intolerant   self righteous   paranoia
hyper vigilance   nightmares
exhaustion   fatigue   lost jobs   lack**

of understanding   overreacting
despair   hopelessness   dominating
insane   psychotic   isolating
grandiose   overeating   bored
impatient   over sleeping   tunnel
vision   distracted   rage   rejection
addictive   desperate   easily
frustrated   denial   blaming   crying
bad reputation   extreme behavior
OCD   state induced recall   animal
abuse   anxiety   tangential   panic
hallucinations   anasognosia   talk
too much   inappropriate   won't
listen   controlling   must be center
stage   all or nothing   don't know
what we want   not accepted   broken
relationships   loss of trust
argumentative   belligerent   blunt
say too much   quitter
overwhelming   scared   avoidance
over sexed   suicidal   no boundaries
poor judgement   misperceptions
con-men   multi-personality
inability to concentrate   abandoned
by family & friends   unreliable   no
privacy   comatose   unable to work
hiding in closet   extensive risk taking

sweet tooth   stronger invitation to act
compulsive   over religious
obsessive   hear voices   irritability
irrational   shopping sprees   hyper-
defensive   dismissive of physical
extreme variance of capacities
hypochondriac   irresponsible   lazy
sleepless   sleep issues   alcohol
drugs   sex   over sensitive   easily
offended   run away   discounted
indecision   lack of trust   no self
esteem   ups and downs   strange
friends   hostility   relationships
medical side effects   memory loss
no impulse control   jobs hard to keep
hard to get up   unable to handle
stress   poor eating habits   boredom
sarcastic   no energy   read too much
critical   hateful   foul mouth
delusions   cutting   unstable
daydream   over commit   no rational
thinking   uncontrollable crying
Seroquel®   lithium   Prozac®
alcoholism   drug abuse   hyper-
sexual   hypo-sexual   racing
thoughts   labeling   out of control
different   sadness   misfit   busy

mind   superiority complex   we
become somebody else   unable to
sleep   can't relate   can't function
manic   over-extending   inability to
move   withdrawn   over spending
can't piece together   need to please
bigger than life   delusional   hear
things   serial relationships   no
sticking to it   we think we are weird
make strange friends   inability to
discuss   fear   inconsistent   start
but don't finish   easily bored
obsessive   expect others to be on our
level   overly happy   contrary
antagonistic   hitting rock bottom
losing touch with reality
uncontrolled temper   very bad
depression   stop making sense
rapid mood swings   confusing others
long depression   can't get out of bed
hopeless   helpless   failure
hospitalizations   medical experiment
weight gain   extreme highs and lows
detached from feelings   not efficient
uncontrollable   impulsive
uncomfortable   ratchet jaw
judgmental   anxious   self doubt

**repetitive   lack of concentration
misunderstood   isolated   over-
confident   sleep too much   extremes
structured   disorganized   frustrated
delusions of grandeur   escapist
excitable   state specific memory
loved and hated at the same time
loved and hated by the same person**

Which items on the list do you relate to? Do you have any to add? Try putting together your own list. You must create your own list if you are going to learn to face it and defeat it instead of continuing to let it defeat you.

My Bad

I am not sure what is worse, the pain I have been through or the pain I have caused others. I am sure I have inflicted way more pain than anyone could handle. But then there are times when I am sure I can't handle my own pain anymore and just want (need) to end it all right now. In case you are offended by the suggestion that there is a Bipolar Advantage let me be very clear - bipolar is the worst kind of hell imaginable.

There are times that are so dark the only option left is to kill myself. It goes on forever and I can't even remember a time when it was not dark. But enough of that for now. Lets talk about the other pain for a while.

When I was 10, I came home from playing baseball, or was it running naked through the park? I can't remember.

The rest I remember like it just happened. The door was locked and my sister Sandy was downstairs listening to music with a friend. She must not have heard me, but I thought she was doing it on purpose. I felt a chill going up my spine and my whole body started to shake uncontrollably. (It still happens to me and I am pretty sure it is an internal feeling, not visible to others.) My mind started racing. I started pounding on the door with all my might and Sandy finally came and opened it up. I started screaming at her and her friend and no matter how they tried to calm me down, I just kept getting worse. It felt like I was possessed by the ultimate evil. They went back downstairs to get away from me, but it was too late. I went to the kitchen drawer and grabbed the biggest knife. I took off after them and chased them around the ping pong table waving the knife and screaming. It was my first memory of going into a rage and I don't remember how I calmed down.

Next thing I can remember, later that day, I am in the garage of a friend down the street laughing about his change in the lyrics of a popular song of the day. I have no idea why that is significant, but there it is. Next thing I am standing with a police officer and he is telling me I am in big trouble. Little did he know how big! I am shaking now, 38 years later, just from the memory, and on the verge of tears at the same time. How do you face the fact that you are such a horrible person?

Sure, we all have lost it at some point in our lives. This is not even remotely the same. I lost it so many times and in so many ways I can't remember even 1% of them. There is always an excuse. Someone started it. Someone said something wrong. Someone didn't agree with me. Or worse,

I imagined someone offended me at such a level that I swear it happened. Paranoid, delusional, hallucinating, all part of my personal hell that spills over on innocent victims.

There are countless memories in my life that to this day I can't sort out whether they actually happened. Were they really talking about me and plotting to destroy me? Were they even there? I remember so many times of flying and floating above the ground that I know I can do it. I remember one time I dreamt I ate a ten pound marshmallow. When I woke up the pillow was gone. Just kidding. Lighten up. If I can accept it so can you. It's my insanity. Lucky for you it is not yours. Even luckier if you have some of your own insanity to hide from the world. You get up the nerve to tell the world on your own. This is my turn.

I really feel sorry for the teachers who were stuck with me. Actually I feel sorry for anyone who has ever met me, but there has to be someone out there who thinks I'm a great guy. I am a fucking genius[1]. 142 I.Q. Smarter than anyone I ever met. Biggest asshole on the planet. Everyone else is an idiot and it is my job to make sure they know it. Slept through class and somehow absorbed the information from the book I was sleeping on. Even woke up one time and ripped the textbook in half in front of the class and told the teacher she was an idiot. Aced every test though, and actually was the smartest person my school had ever seen. And my counselor thought that information would make me less arrogant?

The school system had no idea what to do with me and I had no idea what to do with them. I remember arguing

---

1 http://mednews.stanford.edu/releases/2002/may/creative_gen.html

with my law teacher because he marked one of my answers wrong. I opened the book for the first time ever and turned right to the page that proved me right. He wisely decided that I should correct all the papers and just gave me a blanket 'A' for the course. Even skipped out for lunch with me once on my motorcycle and we got caught by the principal. He actually was the only one who ever stimulated me to learn and he challenged my childish view of reality.

The math department was in for a whole new level of hell. I repeatedly told the teacher he was stupid because he had to do twenty steps to get the answer when there was only one step necessary - ask me. Like I said before, I have no idea why answers just popped into my head. Maybe I am an asshole savant. He tried the same tactic as the law teacher and let me grade the papers. In this case it backfired really badly. I cheated on everyone's grades and pretty much ran the class as my own fiefdom. I even wrote profanity on the chalk board so that when he came in and pulled up the screen everyone would laugh at him. Why didn't anyone figure out that I was crazy? I know, "I'm not crazy. I just have a mood disorder."

I graduated from the education system and moved on to bigger and better things. Well, I actually just quit in my last year of college because I could not take the idiots anymore. (Did I mention delusions of grandeur?)

A whole new level of torment can be inflicted on employees. U-Haul nicknamed me 'The Terminator' because I would go on a rage and fire employees for just 'looking' stupid. And I was an equal opportunity abuser. I cut off a meeting of the top executives of the tech firm I worked for and berated them for 45 minutes. The CEO couldn't take it and had to leave the room for a while. When he came back he offered me a raise. How do I find companies that not only put up with it but encourage my behavior?

I remember going into a half hour rage at my boss once for mentioning what a great job I did with a client. I threatened to shoot everyone in the office. Good thing I was 2000 miles away or I would have chased everyone out of the building. She has never hated anyone so much in her life, but I do know that she took the worst I ever dished out for two years. I still think she is an idiot though.

I lost count of the people I threatened to shoot or to blow up their office or home. Only one deserved it, and he is the one who called the cops on me. Of course I just laughed at the cop and told him he had no proof, so fuck off.

My poor wives. The first one wisely threw me out early on before I actually got too hostile. The second one didn't take so much either, but I'm sure she has a ton of stories to tell her shrink for the rest of her life. Ellen, on the other hand, is a saint. She not only put up with me for fifteen years, but still does. I can't believe how many times I laid on the bullshit about how she doesn't understand I am making everything happen and how she is just in my way. The list of abuses Ellen has had to put up with makes everyone else seem like a wimp for not handling the little amount thrown their way. Not like she doesn't stick up for herself. She is not only an expert at saying just the right thing, she has 'the look' down to a science. We finally decided we hate being apart more than we hate being together and that love is not the warm and happy feeling we sometimes share, but the commitment we have for each other.

How can you wonder what 'the look' means? Didn't your mother ever give it to you?

The incident that haunts me the most, though, is the poor old man I ran into in a parking lot. I was cutting across a parking lot to avoid a traffic light when I blew by this guy at 60 miles an hour. At the last second I decided to stop at the grocery store for some ice cream, so I slammed on the brakes and stopped right in front. Of course, I was not supposed to park in the red zone, but I was more important than anyone else. The old man pulled up as I got out and said "excuse me" which was instantly met with "Fuck you" as I ran into the store to grab the ice cream and cut in front of the line. On the way out the old man came up to me in the store and said "I am so sorry if I bothered you. I am lost and need help finding my house." I jumped in his face and said "What the fuck do I care? Get the hell out of my way!" and stormed out. By the time I got home I realized what a monster I had become and resolved to quit my job and retire so I could go back to the peaceful saintly guy I imagined I really was. The memory of it still haunts me.

How is it possible to think my own pain can even compare? Well, for one, I don't think I ever drove anyone to want to kill themselves, even if they all wished I was dead. Nobody knows the pain that I have endured and it is impossible to explain it. Far better writers than I have tried, but unless you have been there yourself it is like reading that yogurt label. No way do I wish anyone to have a taste of it either. I might be an asshole, but I'm not sadistic.

The greatest pain for me came later in life, which is typical. My earlier bouts with depression were more like being totally drained of energy. I would sleep for months and hardly get out of bed to eat. I thought I had a thyroid problem. I do now, thanks to lithium. Maybe it was mononucleosis or blood sugar issues. Doctors couldn't figure it out. Why couldn't they see that it was manic-depression?

For six months while living in the monastery I was so drained of energy that they had to bring food to my bedroom because I couldn't get up. Although I hated the lack of energy, the emotions I had were of bliss. It wasn't until after my diagnosis that I realized that I was in what they call a mixed state. Part depression, part manic delusion is a state common to many mystics, especially saints in the Catholic church.

I would suddenly be in a fog. Here I was the smartest guy on the planet, and I couldn't even see clearly or break through the fog long enough to complete a thought. For the longest time, I thought I was in a different reality and was experiencing God. Still do. It was actually enjoyable. I would stop breathing and just be there in the moment, sometimes for as along as ten minutes. Only after my diagnosis did I start hating every second of it as a sign of how sick I am. But that is not the pain I am talking about.

The pain I am talking about is the worst state possible. What makes bipolar even worse is to be met with such total lack of understanding by people who actually tell me to 'snap out of it' or 'pick yourself up by your bootstraps'. What the hell were they thinking? It's like being stuck in a moment when your whole body is on fire and someone is holding up a fan to cool you off. It only fans the flame. Only the moment never ends and you can't remember a time before it began.

Sometimes the world becomes so dark it is unbearable. My vision becomes black and white, but mostly just dark grey. My mind repeats thoughts of pain and death over and over and over for hours (and sometimes days). The rage of hate swells up inside, but this time the full fury is directed at me. There is only one way out - suicide, and my mind can't stop plotting ways to do it. And it's not just mental. My whole body aches so bad I can't bear it. And for this they give me a drug that has me slumped over the toilet puking? Did I mention it seems like it goes on forever? Must have been a bipolar Christian who came up with the concept of hell.

Most people cry when they lose a loved one or get an injury. They like to cry when watching a movie and something sad happens. I cry for no reason at all and for every reason. It doesn't do any good, but I can't stop it. I can't even start to cry sometimes on the hope that it will somehow act as a relief valve and help the pain go away temporarily. (Sure I cry from movies. Like the time Arnold stopped making movies and decided to run for office. It's a guy thing. Not sure why though. Was it no more violent flicks or the violence he was going to do to our government? Just kidding. I need a break from such negativity before I get so depressed this book never gets finished.)

Ever since I can remember I have been tormented with thoughts of suicide. "Swerve into oncoming traffic." "Run into that bridge." "Jump off that cliff." "Pull the trigger." "End it now." The thoughts just pop into my head all the time. It is as if there is a little demon in my head that is dying to catch me off guard and get me to actually do it.

It's not painful like the depression but perhaps might be the one thing that finally kills me.

You see there is one thing worse than being with me. 'Being' me is much worse. If you think my mood is unbearable to you, just think how it is for me.

I also have most of the other horrible symptoms ranging from those I can handle to out of control, but then so do most of the people in the workshop once you get them to admit it. But that is for another book. This one is about the Bipolar Advantage, not the Bipolar Disadvantage.

What Is Good About Bipolar?

The first Bipolar Advantage - Brainstorming

I have been teaching brainstorming for 15 years to everyone from kids to college professors to janitors to CEOs and am convinced it is one of the most important skills we can develop. Because our education system seems to place the most emphasis on rote memory and doesn't even mention brainstorming, it is no wonder nobody knows how to do it. Ask successful people and they will tell you that brainstorming is the key to success. Too bad they don't even know how to do it.

You may have been to a meeting where someone says "Let's brainstorm a new idea for..." The group sits around for an hour and debates the relative merit of the three ideas somebody had the courage to offer up for assault. The nay-sayers and over-analyzers pick the idea apart to the point that nobody is going to set himself up to look stupid by offering up another idea. Finally the committee comes to some form of consensus and they all congratulate themselves for how smart they are.

What a bunch of idiots. If you went outside for an hour and three drops of water fell on the entire group would you call that a rain storm? A storm is when you are out for three minutes and you are so drenched a shower would seem drier. Shouldn't a BRAIN storm have the same effect? A brainstorm should produce so many ideas that you can't possibly write them down fast enough. This is one of the major advantages of the bipolar mind. We can brainstorm better than anyone. Why are 'racing thoughts' listed as one of the bad things about the bipolar condition?

Racing thoughts are a terrible thing if you lose control of them, but our greatest asset if we learn their power. The secret is to record them while letting the mind go out of control. Just like mastering golf or any other sport, it takes technique and practice to hone your skill.

So what is this magical technique? How can I change one of the worst things about being bipolar into a Bipolar Advantage? It's easy really. Mostly it's about what NOT to do.

Remember the story about the brainstorming session? What did they do wrong? How could a whole group of people spend an hour and only come up with three ideas and I can come up with a hundred in three minutes all by myself? Why do my ideas blow theirs away? Sure I have delusions of grandeur, but that doesn't mean I'm not right. Learn the technique and hone the skill with practice and I guarantee you will come to the same opinion that this is a major Bipolar Advantage.

First you have to understand a little about how the mind works. Have you ever heard about the two sides of the brain? The left side handles analytical thinking and is practically the only part trained by our education system. You know the three 'R's - reading, writing, and regurgitating. The left brain is at home with verbal skills, math, and logic. Great skills indeed and extremely necessary. They give us the ability to analyze information and make important decisions. They are also the skills that waste an hour to come up with three ideas. The right side of the brain is the creative side. It deals with art, music, visual, tactile, sex, all the fun stuff. It is also the doorway to our subconscious. The right side of the brain is what gives me the ability to come up with 100 ideas in three minutes. It doesn't hurt that I have practiced the techniques and have the Bipolar Advantage.

About the subconscious. Remember the time you spent all day trying to figure something out and you were standing in the shower rubbing yourself? (You weren't using a washcloth, were you? It's so impersonal.) So your mind is focused on cleaning your genitals and all of a sudden 'Wham', the answer pops in your head. You don't even think "where'd that come from?" You just stopped what you were doing and rushed to write it down before you forgot it. You did write it down, didn't you? How many times does the subconscious tell us answers before we figure out we won't remember them when we wake up? O.K. So it didn't happen for you in the shower. Whatever floats your boat. Maybe it was while playing golf, watching a movie, making love. Whatever it was, you know it happened. You see, I think this is where all the answers came from when I was in school. The subconscious mind knows everything. The key is to figure out how to hear it tell you the answers.

So what does this have to do with left brain - right brain? And why do bipolars have an advantage? The right brain is the door to our subconscious. All of the great ideas, not to mention every answer in the universe, come from our subconscious. When we are not stuck in the left brain analyzing our thoughts to death, the creative side has a chance to work. Don't worry, there is plenty of time later to throw out all the stupid ideas before you tell anyone. When we find ourselves relaxing into our hobbies, having sex, taking a shower, daydreaming, or whatever relaxes us, our subconscious has a chance to get our attention.

The activities that open our mind to the subconscious are always right brain things. The important thing is to not be having sex with your partner and in the middle of "ooh - ooh" suddenly stop and say "ah-hah". The point is, learning how to turn off the left brain and let the right side have access to the subconscious can be the most important lesson you will ever learn.

The diagram on the facing page is a generally accepted illustration of left and right brain functions. Note that the right brain seems to be where the subconscious thoughts and ideas become conscious.

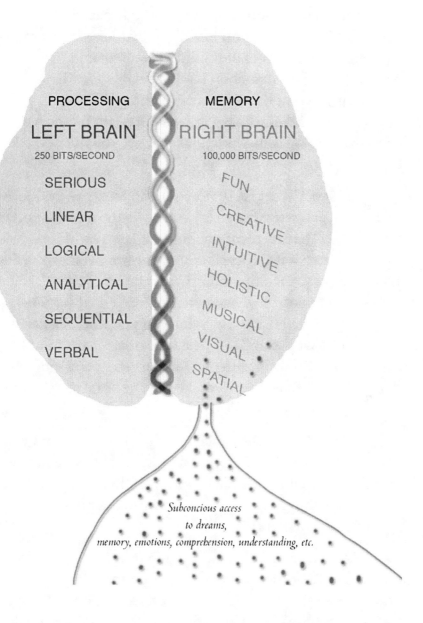

PROCESSING

MEMORY

LEFT BRAIN

RIGHT BRAIN

250 BITS/SECOND

100,000 BITS/SECOND

SERIOUS

FUN

LINEAR

CREATIVE

LOGICAL

INTUITIVE

ANALYTICAL

HOLISTIC

SEQUENTIAL

MUSICAL

VERBAL

VISUAL

SPATIAL

Subconcious access
to dreams,
memory, emotions, comprehension, understanding, etc.

So what is the technique and why are bipolars at an advantage? Have more sex. And tell your partner (or yourself if that is how you like it) that you are trying to use it to brainstorm. It works, but I didn't teach that in corporations. Did I mention bipolar people tend to be promiscuous? Another Bipolar Advantage? Depends on how you look at it. You just have to create the conditions for success by doing something that will get you out of the left brain.

First off, what NOT to do. Do not analyze the ideas that come, just write them down. This is the most important thing of all. There is plenty of time for analysis of the ideas later. Sit down with a pencil and paper (or a voice recorder if you are alone). Set a timer for three minutes. I assure you this is all you need and even the best can't do it for much longer. Pick a topic. We use "what can you find in a grocery store" in the workshop. It is best to use easy topics until you are well practiced. Start the timer. Start writing. Remember, don't analyze. Every time you let the left brain step in you waste time and might miss the most important idea.

Ding. Time's up. Pencils down. How many did you get? Did you get the most? For a group that has delusions of grandeur I would guess they would all think they came out first. Funny thing is people seldom raise their hand even in my bipolar workshops.

So you say I didn't answer the question "Why do bipolars have an advantage?" Are you bipolar? Compare your number to someone who is not. Not bipolar? Too bad. At least you don't have to put up with the bad things. All alone? Don't worry, I have been doing this for a long time. In most corporate and educational environments, the people are so stuck in the left brain that they only average 7 items on the list. If you couldn't beat 7, you should have your diagnosis checked.

How can you spend three minutes listing items in a grocery store and only come up with seven items? Easy. Take milk. Does it belong in the store? Where is it kept? What temperature does it have to be kept at? How many different kinds are there? How much does it sell for? Who gives a shit. We are trying to make a list of items, not figure them out. The reason a group comes up with three ideas in an hour is because they spend so much time trying to prove that every idea is a bad one.

Milk - whole milk, low fat, chocolate, soy, acidophilus, powdered, lactose intolerant, 2%, 1%, cow milk, goat milk, cheese, yogurt, ice cream, cookies, pie, steak, sexy blonde at the cash register. I got 18 in the time it took some people to work to the price in the analysis that should have been left out. And what about those items that are not related to milk? I don't know about you, but the best place to find sex is in the grocery store so tell me you never saw a sexy blonde at the cash register? Remember, we are trying to make a list so our brain can learn to storm, not analyze the ideas for quality.

Why do bipolars have an advantage? Because when we figure out that it is both a disadvantage AND an advantage to have a mind that runs wild, we find that we are wired for success at least in brainstorming.

The average bipolar gets 45 answers. So how many of the answers are crazy? Who cares. If you take ten bipolars and they average 45 each you have 450 ideas in three minutes. You now have 57 minutes to sort them out. Throw away all the bad ones and you are down to a list of ten great ideas. I know from experience that the ten bipolar ideas are way better than the three lame excuses the corporate hacks came up with.

Once I teach this to corporations the equation changes. They start to average twenty each. They also are not afraid to share first and analyze later. They get to laugh at the weird ones. They call me the next day and tell me about the idea they had in the shower last night. I ask "was it good for you?" The bipolar wacko who torments them all suddenly has status. His ideas are listened to. They let him abuse the management and employees and still keep his job. So that's why they let me get away with so much at my jobs, do ya think?

Companies are desperate for good ideas. My good idea makes us more competitive. Our new bipolar company is going to rule the world. Better keep some accountants around before we waste all the money on shower massagers in the rest rooms though.

Why do I get 100 when the average bipolar gets 45? Practice. It doesn't hurt to have the delusion that I am smarter than everybody, even if sooner or later I find out that I'm dead wrong.

Important points to remember:

Sometimes the mind takes you down a path of relationships to help you see the best ideas.

Quantity, not quality is the most important principal.

After the storm you can sort out the good ideas.

Why do so many people who have changed the world say the idea came to them in the shower?

Look at the bright side of life

You've heard the stories. A man had a terrible accident and somehow turned it into a positive thing in his life. A woman lost her sight and made hearing her strength. A mother lost her child in a car accident and created an organization against drunk drivers. We all have things to overcome in our lives. It may seem like our life is hell, but you can always find someone worse off that found the bright side of life.

You've done it yourself. If you look hard enough there must be a time when you overcame some kind of adversity. What was it? If even in the smallest way, nobody makes it through life without overcoming something. A wise person once said "I have come to measure spiritual advancement, not alone by the light that surrounds one when he meditates or by the visions he has of saints, but by what he is able to endure in the hard, cold light of day.[1]" By that measure, the ability to endure the hell of bipolar makes us great souls indeed.

There's more to it than that, though. When I was managing a retirement home, there was a woman living there named Martha Stein, who I will never forget.

1 Sri Gyanamata, God Alone, The life and Letters of a Saint, page 181. Los Angeles: Self Realization Fellowship, 1984

Whenever I would relate my troubles to her, she would remind me that everything that happens to us is neither bad nor good. It is we who choose to put a value on it, so choose to find the good in it. It seems like such a simplistic view of life, but in reality it is not only very wise, it is incredibly hard sometimes to put into practice. I was at her side when she died and she smiled against the ultimate loss. If Martha can smile in the face of death, I can find the good in at least some of my issues.

How many times do we choose to see the bad in situations? How many of the items in the bad list could be looked at from the bright side? Is the racing mind a curse, or is it just a condition that we can hone into an advantage? If conditions were responsible for happiness, then the same car or the same clothes would make us all happy. It would be a pretty boring world, too. Those of us who learn to look for the bright side of life in everything, sometimes even surprise ourselves that it turns out to be true.

The good things about bipolar

"This is bullshit. There is nothing good about being bipolar." We are so stuck looking at the dark side that we get upset about the possibility that there might be brightness on the other side. I'm not saying that bipolar is the greatest thing in the world. I already said it is the worst kind of hell. But to deny that it has good features is to deny reality. You see, I'm on a mission to get bipolar out of the closet and into the bedroom. Or should I have said the boardroom? It is just as unhealthy to pretend the bad does not exist as it is to deny the good. People call me the 'Pied Piper of Crazy.' Well if that is what it takes to get even one person to start seeing life as it really is, then it is worth all the hostility I can bear. I have already seen many people start on the path to a better life with bipolar. I hope I can convince you to take that path too.

You don't even have to look at the bright side of hardship to see some great things about being bipolar. It may seem like a shock, but every time I lead a workshop through a brainstorming exercise and we play a game about looking for the bright side of life, we end up making a bigger list of positives than the negative list I wrote about earlier.

Of course I cheat just a little. I never mention that you could learn how to brainstorm before making the bad list. I never told everyone they could choose to look at the bad side of life, either. I figure we have had plenty of practice doing that.

Some of the greatest people in history were bipolar[1]. For the workshop I searched the internet for famous bipolars and came up with an incredible list. Christopher Columbus, Virginia Woolf, Abraham Lincoln, Florence Nightingale, Andrew Carnegie, and of course Vincent van Gogh to name a few.

Although I have been looking for years for anything that would look at the bright side of bipolar, there has seldom been anyone willing to stick their neck out and challenge the presumption that bipolar is all bad. Recently a great book came out by a researcher at Johns Hopkins University Medical School named John D. Gartner, Ph. D.

---

1 http://www.bipolarsupport.org/famous.html

His book is called 'The Hypomanic Edge - The link between a little craziness and a lot of success in America'[1].

Gartner said that it was people with our traits who had the creativity, drive, and willingness to take great risks and who were willing to give up everything and move to our country to start a new life. They passed those traits on to us and now we have the same opportunity for greatness. His stories detailing the lives of great people in history are very inspirational.

I loved the book so much I put it down and got right on this book that I have been wanting to write for a long time. I got to this point in the first draft in three days, and last week I hadn't been out of bed in three months. How's that for a change in attitude?

The following traits were called out by the participants of the workshop as good things they associate with bipolar. These are not the clinical items you find in a textbook. These items are what help real patients feel better about themselves whether they are associated with bipolar or not.

starting over   reckless behavior   all or nothing   successful accomplished   takes 2 - 3 to replace us blunt   over sexed   sense of humor perfect timing   sex   run away strange friends   relationships

---

1 Gartner, John D. The Hypomanic Edge - The link between a little craziness and a lot of success in America New York: Simon & Schuster, 2005

daydream   hyper-sexual   racing
thoughts   different   creativeness
busy mind   can do anything   bigger
than life   delusional   make strange
friends   efficient   intense
concentration   happiness   creative
intelligent   sensitive   perceptive
mania under control   fresh and
growing mind   increased creativity
more energy   insightful   dance
more   more music   enthusiasm
get more done   adventure   feel more
depression saves money   this too
shall pass   extra attention   perfect
excuse   good lover   passionate
write more letters   more tolerant
we are necessary   never boring
artistic   mind slows down   put
totally unrelated things together
more alive   more interesting   meet
interesting people   are interesting
people   delusions of grandeur
positive   can work non-stop
focused   obsessive   great sense of
humor   energetic   empathetic
good listeners   motivational   non-
judgmental   starters   musical

famous   articulate   coping skills
risk takers   set priorities   aware of
feelings   happy   good at sales
good actors   good therapists
inventive   active fantasy life
escapist   good supporter   mediators
love   manifestor   high on life
involved   customer service   sales
communication   flexible   available
unique   deep (not shallow)   fun
open minded   friendly   sociable
life of the party   charismatic
talented   productive   innovators
encyclopedic   voracious learner
explorers   adventurers   multi-
dimensional   rich lives   interesting
tenacity   creativity   determination
prepared   endless energy   athletic
dramatic   counselor   good manager
financially successful   planner
brainstormer   can fit in with all
make good psychiatrists   good
cleaners   good organizers   designers
loyal   dreamers   willing to try the
unconventional   more intense
outperform   more accepting
humorous   write better

knowledgeable patient   resourceful
willing and helpful   handle sticky
situations   visual   sense of self
ability to laugh at one's self
automatic self starter   entertaining
constant companionship
contemplative   more aware   funnier
cheerful   we know other bipolars
bipolars attract   tolerant   job
security by talent   entrepreneurial
natural high   introspective
extroverted   take charge   volunteer
pathologically helpful   courageous
survivors   brave   experimenting
auditioning   childlike   comedic
sympathetic   silly   uninhibited
hijinks organizer   outgoing
generous   always new   organized
effervescent   committed   multi-
interests   multi-tasking   mega-
talented   real   honest   tell it like it
is   confident   jack of all trades
master of facts   talkative
Pollyannaish   optimistic   caretakers
compassionate   variety   not boring
lively   personable   multi sensory
input   psychic   spontaneous

upbeat   informative   high speed
charming   leader   magnetic
theatrical   excitable   spiritual
fearless   happy   ecstatic   sexual
engaging   infectious   affectionate
kind   loving   witty   outside the
box   daring   rapid thoughts
pressured speech   people want our
ideas   over the top   loyal to our faith
insatiable   lust for life   state specific
memory   ability to learn   experience
the spiritual   street drugs
unnecessary   ability to confront
reality   intuitive   balanced
natural advocates   do-gooders
loved and hated at the same time
loved and hated by the same person
game for anything   inspiring   not
afraid of death   singers   writers
poets   able to cry   emotional
knowledge   emotionally motivated
actors   actresses   our lives are good
stories   we tell stories well   playing
God's role for us

Which items on the list do you relate to? Do you have any to add? Try putting together your own list. Your list of good traits is what you can turn to when you think all is lost.

In the workshop it is amazing how many items that we list as bad end up on the good list too. How many items on the bad list can you see also on the good list? How many on the good list could be on the bad? It's not all black and white. People say "Life sucks and then you die," but somewhere along the way you learn to see the beauty.

Lucky Me

Sometimes I think I am the luckiest guy in the world. I have had such an amazing life. I wouldn't trade it for anyone's. I can't believe what mediocrity and boredom people settle for. I have had so many different careers I lost count. Talk about variety: prostitute, drug dealer, factory worker, traveling waiter, health club manager, corporate vice president, male stripper, truck driver, monk, teacher, public speaker, trade show hawker, car salesman, body builder, computer programmer, realtor, creative director, tech guru, porn star, this list goes on and on.

When you change careers every nine months you get to try out a lot of them. When you're manic you learn new skills and succeed at them extremely fast too. And I made money. Retired a multimillionaire at 42. To be just rich, or just the CEO of a company, and miss out on all the variety would have been so boring I would have killed myself by now.

Having bipolar took away the inhibitions that would have kept me from doing many of the fun things that I did. I was never bogged down with what I 'should' or 'shouldn't' do. There are very few things I have not at least tried unless they are similar to other things that I tried before and didn't like.

Thought I was talking to God most of the time. Still do. One morning in the monastery I was sitting at breakfast and had a flashback to a time when I ate 28 grams of mushrooms. (Most people eat 1 or 2 grams.) My instant thought was that I am so much higher than that now and I didn't have to take anything to get there. The high from meditation is better than anything; no amount of drugs can compare.

There is a point when even your heart stops that every culture in the world talks about. They call it ecstasy, nirvana, samadhi, bliss, and a hundred other terms. Saint Paul said he died daily. That state of breathless bliss is what he was talking about. Been there off and on since I was 2. Got there a million ways. Brought lots of people there having sex with them. Makes everything else seem like nothing. Ain't it great to be crazy?

One thing about bipolars, we are the life of the party. Just don't go too far; there is a fine line between 'fun' and 'asshole' and we have little (or no) control over it.

Remember I talked about losing it and screaming at people? One time I was in an auto shop and another rage started coming on. And for good reason - they were blatantly in the wrong. I stopped right there and said "You don't understand. I am on medication for being crazy and you are pushing me over the edge. One more minute and we are both going to hate it. The police will have to come and it will not be pretty." As I drove away I became so happy. For the first time in my life I figured out what to do because I knew what was going on. Because I came to face who I really am, I gained the insight to act correctly at least that time. I use the technique now whenever I want to cut in line at the pharmacy. I hold up my lithium bottle and announce that I am starting to lose it. What a dick. (Did I mention delusional?)

Talk about having energy. At 37 years old I bought my first computer. In six months I learned the basics of UNIX, Windows, and Mac OS, downloaded web pages and taught myself to make my own, learned programming, and in six months started charging $800 a day to teach technology to Fortune 500 companies all over the world. During that time my typical day was to read a tech manual, play on the computer, work out for three hours, race my boat, smoke pot, walk naked through my admiring audience while they stuffed $20 bills in my socks while fondling my rock hard body, went out and danced all night long, and laid in bed for a couple hours plotting my future before getting up and doing it all again. Manic Depression has given me the ability to do great things in my life, or at least the delusion to think they were!

Sure I have morals. I have never been in a physical fight. I actually think verbal abuse is just as bad, and am learning to control that too. I almost always apologize for my behavior. I try to make up for it when I say mean things. Most importantly, I love myself and accept myself for who I really am. That doesn't mean I have not spent my life trying to improve, but that is for a later topic.

But the good of bipolar isn't what we get away with, it is the strengths we gain from facing ourselves. When people share their deepest feelings with us, they intuitively know we understand, and they feel at ease telling us what they hide from everyone else. And we DO know how it feels. Most people don't have a clue what to do when confronted with shared emotional pain. We are the experts. We can handle hardships like nobody else. We do all the time - it's called bipolar. It gives us tremendous strength and perspective.

We are more aware of emotions than anybody else because we have such a tremendous range of them. The doctors try to keep us in a state of numbness for fear we will go too far, but if we could just cut off the worst at both ends we would have a richness of experience that makes normalcy dull and boring. Normalcy IS boring even if we do suffer the extremes some times.

Just like I suffer from most of the traits on the bad list, I enjoy the good ones too. The bipolar mind turns off the filter that says we shouldn't or can't do something. It has helped me to live an incredibly diverse and exciting life.

It's bad, it's good, so what?

Whether you can put value judgments on traits and label some bad and some good is not really the point. It is that we make an honest assessment of who we really are. We don't hide behind "woe is me" or deny things about ourselves that are so apparent to everyone around us. For literally every person who has taken the Bipolar Advantage Workshop, it has been a huge awakening to actually build a list of traits and start the next step in learning how to make the best of it. Each participant said "I learned so much about myself from doing the exercises and am glad for it," or something similar. To know who we really are is the first step to changing ourselves into a better version. But the process of change is for a later chapter. First we have to talk about acceptance.

Acceptance

Acceptance is the key to starting on the journey of healing. Do you know someone who truly accepts you just the way you are? Do you accept someone else just the way he/she is? Do you even accept yourself the way you are? In order to help someone else grow or to grow ourselves, we must learn to accept exactly who we really are, not who we pretend to be. Only by discovering who we really are, accepting ourselves and others, and loving ourselves in spite of our flaws, can we learn and grow to be better people. This is why one of the basic tenets of marriage is to "love you just the way you are."

We all wish others would accept and love us. We wish we could just be ourselves and not have to hide behind a false front. To achieve that, we need to accept and love ourselves as well as accept and love others. One of the Bipolar Advantages that is illustrated so well in bipolar support groups is our ability to accept others, and support them in spite of their traits that we are so intimately familiar with.

No matter what the issue, you cannot even start to work on it until you accept it. That does not mean surrender to it. You need to admit to yourself that this trait really is a part of you and you can still love yourself in spite of it, while trying your best to be a better person. It takes tremendous strength to admit to yourself that you have both good and bad traits that could use some tweaking. Unless you come to acceptance, everybody else will know the truth about you in spite of how well you hide it from yourself. By looking at the things we judge as bad and balancing them with the ones we see as good, we can come to love ourselves and start on the path of making the good outweigh the bad instead of the bad covering up the good.

Let me repeat, acceptance does not mean surrender. To surrender is to say "There is nothing I can do about it so I might as well keep doing it." To accept is to give it our best effort while not compounding the problem with thoughts and emotions like guilt and blame that only make it worse. Acceptance is to love yourself for who you are today while striving to be the person you can love even more tomorrow.

Do you love everything about yourself? Why not? Do you even admit to yourself who you really are? Most of us don't. Do you know anyone who would love you unconditionally no matter what secret you let out? Are you afraid to talk about a part of you with anybody? Are you afraid to find out about it yourself so you just live in fear and denial about your own thoughts and actions? Don't you think that's sad?

How can we learn to better accept ourselves? Easier to start out learning to accept others. If someone says something to you, do you give them a look or response that makes them feel like telling you more? Or less? Do you make judgments about other people's traits? Do you do the same for your own traits? It is easier to accept the things you don't like in others since you don't have to live with them internally. You don't identify with them. What things about people do you disapprove of? Once you build a list you might find you have a lot of those traits yourself. If you can accept that somebody else has a particular trait, maybe you can accept it in yourself.

We also need to start accepting our circumstances. It works the same way. We need to learn to make the best of every situation while striving to make it better. Fighting our own negativity adds a huge burden to a situation that is hard enough on it's own. Remember, acceptance does not mean surrender.

Acceptance is most important of all

How many examples do you know of where someone is in denial and claims that reality is going just fine when it is not true? How can you expect things to get better when you don't even admit that something is wrong? You cannot make something better when you have convinced yourself that there is nothing wrong in the first place. Claiming something is not there does not make it go away, it only makes it stronger. Acceptance of reality is the most important step of all. No progress or action is possible until you take that crucial step.

Introduction to your real self

We have all met somebody new and were fascinated with every detail of his life. It is so interesting to hear where he has been, what he has done, what great tales of sadness and joy he has to share. But unless we accept that person and encourage him to share, we sooner or later start to feel that something is missing. There are great stories that he won't share. We cannot truly know him because he is afraid we won't like that part of himself that he keeps hidden. Well let me introduce you to someone who is the most fascinating person you ever met, yourself.

Do you really know yourself? The process of self awareness might be the hardest thing you have ever done, but you will find it is also the greatest. Start out slow. Look at the easy stuff. Keep a journal. Personal acceptance is something you work on for the rest of your life. By accepting who you really are, you learn to love yourself and to love and accept others too. Other people begin to love and accept you, as you love and accept them.

I love my self

I said in the part about my bad things that I hate myself and so does everyone else. I don't think others accept some of the things that I said were good either. And to think I only let out the things that I thought would only offend half of you! I think I tell sensitive information about myself so that maybe someone will accept it and it will help me to better accept myself. If you can accept me, please let me know. I need all the encouragement I can get.

But I do love myself. As hard as it is, I have been working on my own acceptance for a long time. In many ways I have become a wonderful person who cares to make a positive difference in the world. There are many people who love and admire me, at least until they read this book and find out how fucked up I am. I am gambling that they will love me more for admitting it.

Even in some of my darkest moments there is a part of me that shines through. I sincerely apologize when I do wrong. I am the most accepting of others of anyone I have ever met. Just ask my daughter. We have a love that everyone praises. As I have become more accepting of others and worked on loving myself, I have become a better person.

Are there things I wish I never did? Of course. There are just as many opportunities for greatness that I missed. I admit that I am perhaps the most messed up person you have ever heard about. I have done wrongs that perhaps even Jesus can't forgive. I don't forgive myself either, but I am trying my best to face them and become a better person. For that effort I love myself. I love myself every time the rage wells up and I only scream a little. I love myself when I resist the temptation to do the worst things imaginable and only do the horrible. I love myself when I do the ultimate good to another person and accept her for who she really is. I love myself for who I am today just as much as I am going to love the better person that I strive to be. I accept that I am not perfect while maintaining the hope that I can be. I love that I am bipolar. It has enabled me to see who I really am.

Do you love your self?

Who are you?

What do you accept about yourself?

What do you not accept about yourself?

What vision do you have of a better self?

Why is acceptance the most important of all?

Do you truly love yourself?

Are you ready to start the journey to becoming a better person?

How do you see yourself as a better person?

Introspection

The only way to know who you really are

Introspection is the most important element in putting bipolar 'in order' instead of 'disorder.' Actually, it is the most important element in putting any life in order. If life is a journey and your plans are your map, then introspection is how you know where you are on the map. If someone hands you a map the first thing you do is look for or ask where you are on it. That is introspection.

Every action we take is preceded by a thought. You cannot lift your arm, walk, speak, or even sleep without first thinking about it. As we learn the techniques of introspection and put them into practice, we start to recognize the thoughts that precede everything we do. By recognizing them we have the power to change the direction of the action while we still have control over it. Introspection helps us to control our thoughts and actions before they get out of hand.

Through introspection we become aware of who we are, what we are thinking, and how we are acting, instead of who we imagine ourselves to be. We then can take out our life map, pinpoint exactly where we are on it, and set the course for becoming who we want to be. Along the way we discover that some of the traits that we thought were so bad are really Bipolar Advantages that just needed to be developed and put to proper use. Without introspection we are just drifting aimlessly through a life of disorder, not knowing who we are or where we are going.

The techniques are very easy to understand and put into use. No complicated charts and rules to follow. No replacing this thought by looking it up on a chart and applying a complex analysis. We simply learn to be aware of our thoughts through an easy process. All the questions you need to ask yourself are already in your mind. The process just helps you organize your own questions and helps you find your own answers. Once you learn to look within, you will find that your greatest love has been right there all along - yourself. You also find that you have great gifts to share: acceptance, love, and the awareness of who you really are. Introspection will help you see the advantage of having the wider range of experiences and emotions associated with being bipolar and how to use that advantage in your daily life.

Why Introspect?

Introspection is one of the key practices fundamental to all the major religions. Jesus said that "the kingdom of God is within you[1]." Introspection is the process of looking within to find our soul, the image of the divine in ourselves.

---

1 Luke 17:21

By looking within we come to know who we really are, instead of who we imagine ourselves to be.

Our personal relationship with our soul and God is unique to every one of us. Our spiritual path helps us in establishing that relationship and sets the standards for who we can become through the examples of the great saints and sages. The great teachers of every religion emphasize the importance of being true to our faith. Examining our thoughts and actions in regard to our beliefs is a key to establishing a direct relationship with our true self.

It also doesn't hurt that the more we introspect the better we feel about ourselves.

How do I do it?

Before you leave the house you take a shower, shave whatever part is appropriate, and stand naked in front of the mirror. You make your hair perfect, check that there is nothing stuck in your teeth, check your face, and if you can stand it you take a look at your body. You get dressed, check the mirror again, and take your ugly interior life out in public to ruin the whole effort.

Don't get me wrong. Good grooming is important. I don't like it when my date has green junk in her teeth and her perfume overwhelms the room. I never go back for a second date. I hate it worse when she tailgates and bitches at the slow drivers ahead and is totally unaware that she is doing it. I take a cab home as soon as the car stops. What good is it to INSPECT the outside and forget to INTROSPECT about what we act like.

If you start to pay attention to your actions you will see that we all see the trouble coming up. You're driving down the road of life and you see the thing that always sets you off. Some call it a trigger. So what do you do? You keep heading right for it until it causes the exact same reaction you always have. Admit it. You can accept it. We learned about acceptance in the last chapter. It happens over and over again until we figure out how to handle it right. So what would happen if you saw it coming and decided to take a different route? What if you choose to react differently when the trigger happens? Bingo. You've started to grow. Doesn't mean you will succeed at first, but you will never grow until you take the first step.

O.K. So how do we do it? It is really easy, but it is a little complicated to set up the first time. Setting it up is part of the process, though. What we need is a list of questions to ask ourselves every night. Write down five to seven questions about your thoughts, five to seven about your actions, and if you are of a spiritual nature five to seven about your spiritual practice.

Time to Brainstorm

How do you come up with the list. BRAINSTORM. You have been practicing, haven't you?

Here's a list to get you started:

Thoughts:
1. Was I on a path of improvement today?

2. Did I look for the bright side of life?
3. Did I pay attention to my thoughts throughout the day?
4. Did I try to accept others today?
5. Did I accept myself?
6. Did I try to look for a different way to handle my triggers?
7. Did I think about the effect I have on others?

Actions:
1. Did I react today in the same old way?
2. Did I tell someone I love him/her?
3. Did I yell at anyone?
4. Did I do that thing I am trying to stop doing?
5. Did I exercise today?
6. Did I get out of bed?
7. Did I at least inspect my teeth?

Spiritual Practice:
1. Did I read my spiritual book?
2. Did I meditate for five minutes?
3. Did I seek forgiveness?

4. **Did I pray?**
5. **Did I seek the help of a higher power?**
6. **Did I accept others?**
7. **Did I show love and compassion?**

A little harder than the grocery list, but you can do it. Take the time right now to put your own list together or just write down mine. We need it to do the introspection.

Pick a time that you can sit down for two minutes every day and read the list. If you don't have two minutes to spare stop reading this book. You are wasting your time.

That's it. Nothing complicated. You cannot imagine how powerful it is.

Okay, we both know there are some of you who won't actually do this. For you, there's the workshop.

I promise introspection will change your life forever. How do I know that? Because whenever I give the workshop, people always tell me that this was the easiest and best thing they have ever done. How can two minutes of asking yourself simple questions change your life? Because when the trigger pops up, the subconscious mind will know you are going to ask yourself how you handled it when you introspect tonight. Your subconscious mind watches every thought and action 24 hours a day to help you answer your questions, so you are really practicing introspection constantly. You will quickly find that you become aware of the triggers early enough to choose a different course, and you start making better choices.

All you have to do is ask the right questions. I don't know what they are for you. Everybody is different. The hard part is to start admitting to yourself what you think and do that you want to change. Then put it on your list of questions and you are now on the road to perfection.

Just make sure you don't change the questions every day. It takes at least ten days to turn each question into a subconscious habit. You should make a list, stick with it until it becomes a habit, and change one item at a time. That way, you can keep up your introspection habit without too much upheaval. Also, start out with easy things. Don't work on the really bad stuff until you have some experience that introspection works. You might have to work on the hard stuff for a long time before you beat it, but with introspection and determination you eventually will.

You don't even have to write down the answers, but if you keep a journal you will learn some very interesting things about yourself. You can add comments about the events of the day and how you were doing along with the questions and answers. Next year when the same stuff comes up you can look back and see what you tried that helped you deal with it better. Journaling is a lot of work though. I would not want it to get in the way of doing the introspection. A few minutes a day will change your life. Try it right now.

Remember:

Thoughts lead to all actions.

Five to seven questions each - thoughts, actions, spiritual life.

Keep same questions at least 10 days.

Set regular time for introspection.

Habit makes your subconscious mind aware all of the time.

Software for the Soul

When I retired, I wrote a software program called 'Introspection' (www.soulsoftware.com) that helps you to keep track of your efforts. It has pre-set questions for the five major religions of the world that were written by the clergy of the various faiths; Buddhism, Christianity, Hinduism, Islam, and Judaism. You can follow their suggestions or change them to your own and the program will always remember what you were asking yourself on any date you used it.

'Introspection' by SoulSoftware provides the tools to help you achieve these goals. It offers questions based on your own religion to help you examine your thoughts, your actions, and your spiritual life. You can use the questions provided or rewrite and personalize them.

'Introspection's' journal has the unique advantage of being searchable. When faced with a difficult 'test' you can look back and see how you handled the situation in the past. You can see not only your writings, but also what questions you were asking yourself and the inspirational quotes you read at the time. By looking back you can perceive the wisdom or folly of how you react to life.

We all need inspiration in our lives. Inspiration and guidance from the great religions of the world help us to see more clearly how to do what is right and make the best choice in every circumstance. 'Introspection's' daily quotes illuminate the most meaningful themes for a balanced spiritual life - divine love, peace, forgiveness, wisdom, habits, courage, happiness, and 30 more. As you focus on each topic for ten days or longer, you gain a greater perspective. You can find more information about 'Introspection' software at www.bipolaradvantage.com.

My Interior Life

I have been well aware of my thoughts and actions since early childhood. I think it was a natural result of my obsession with watching my breath. Since I was fascinated with how my breath related to my thoughts and actions it made me very aware of at least the internal consequences of everything I did. So why did I choose to do things when I knew the negative result it would produce? I thought it was fun to feel excited, agitated, calm, still, breathless, electrical, and every other sensation and I did whatever I knew would produce the desired result whether society approved of it or not.

I didn't learn about the type of introspection I am talking about here until my early twenties. It did help me to improve in many ways and I actually did develop some very good traits over the years. I have been very serious about becoming a better person, and even spent two years in a monastery working on it. I have downplayed it so far in this book, because I wanted to illustrate the bad person that I have also been.

Trouble is, the bipolar condition was in my way. I struggled against the desires for inappropriate sex, inappropriate behavior, and inappropriate life, and I could not figure out what was making it so hard. If only I had been diagnosed earlier...

I took the diagnosis that I am bipolar very hard. All the excuses went away and I had to face the fact that I really don't like myself or what I have become. I always thought that I was this wonderful spiritual guy who really wanted to be a saint but was just distracted by a few things that didn't matter anyway. I just haven't been able to resist temptation yet. Maybe you have some idea of how frustrating it is to wish you were somebody better but can't seem to make it happen. The diagnosis changed all that.

It was so hard to come face to face with who I really am for the first time. I had to admit that there is something seriously wrong with me and it is not everyone else's fault. I had to accept that I may never become the saint that I wish I was. I blamed God. I denied God. I hated God. I still don't know what to think of the whole spiritual path. I grew to hate myself. I hated life. I became hopelessly depressed.

The diagnosis was also the greatest relief. It is currently the most significant moment of my life. When I look back later it may lose some of the significance, but it will always be a moment in time that changed everything for me. Hard as it was, I finally had a reason for everything that had happened to me. I don't even care if it turns out I am not bipolar (not a chance) because the diagnosis is nothing but a framework for me to work with. It is not an excuse for my behavior. It is what I have to overcome if I am ever going to achieve my goal to be a better person.

Throughout my life, I have been extremely successful for a while and then it all falls apart. I know just what to do, I just can't seem to sustain the effort and I fall right back into the old patterns. Now I know why. It is part of my condition. I know from experience that if I keep up the habits that work, I become a completely different and better person. I've been there. I have had feedback to make sure it is not just another delusion. I can be a wonderful person all the time. I just need to understand what I am up against so that I can battle against it. I now know what it is.

It took a long time to come to acceptance. After a couple of years I came to say that if I had my life to live all over again I would choose bipolar. Not sure that is true, but to me it means that I have accepted it. It means that I accept myself and love myself for who I REALLY am, a mentally ill guy who desires to be a saint and just can't quite get it together yet. I didn't love myself for a long time, since well before my diagnosis. I do now.

Before the diagnosis, I bought an estate that was owned by a famous healer, Dr. Bernard Jensen. It was next door to the monastery I had lived in years before. People from all over the world had come here and to the monastery to be healed of physical, mental, and spiritual woes. I knew I was moving here because I wanted the life back that I had experienced in the monastery. It was the best I had ever been and I didn't realize I left it because of bipolar depression. I moved to the estate because I didn't love myself anymore and I wanted to return to the place where I remembered being the person I loved. I had no idea at the time that this was going to be the place of my own healing on all three levels; physical, mental, and spiritual. The diagnosis of bipolar was the key that unlocked the whole journey.

I had a great foundation to build on. I already knew the concepts of acceptance, introspection, meditation, and right living. I had been practicing them for a lifetime. Now I knew why I was unsuccessful even though I did make great gains sometimes. I became the president of the local chapter of DBSA, the Depression and Bipolar Support Alliance. I started running support groups where I would help people to at least let out their issues in an environment that made them feel supported. I attended support groups run by others. I read everything I could find. I pulled together everything I had from seminars I had given in the past, from my spiritual life, and from everywhere I could. I put together a workshop more for my own good than to help others. I got started on the path to making bipolar an advantage even though I thought at the time that there was no advantage.

I called the workshop 'Bipolar In Order' because I thought nobody would listen to somebody claiming it is an advantage. I still think Bipolar Advantage is an audacious claim, but I want to make it anyway because if you don't turn it into an advantage you lose.

The first course I gave changed my life. I realized that what I had put together was my own personal recipe for success. I needed the participants to verify it as much as I wanted them to be helped by it. It helped me and the participants far beyond my wildest dreams. I found my purpose in life. Of all the things I have ever done this is the one that means the most to me. More than anything I want this to be the career of my lifetime. It is calling me. I need all the help I can get and am hoping that someone sees the value of my effort and offers support.

Introspection has worked a miracle on me this time. I have not raged at anyone in close to two years now. Compare that to my daily and sometimes hourly outbursts and my victims will tell you it is a miracle. My sexual indiscretions are under control. My moods are in a range that I want them to be in, even if not always under my control. My life is improving on every front. People love and care about me. My marriage is deeper and stronger than ever. I am making a positive difference in many lives. I am becoming a better person every day. I am starting to think once again that it may be possible to become the person I always wished I was.

Am I there yet? No way. I have so far to go I often think it is too late. There are so many things to make up for that I am overwhelmed. I still spend way too much time in bed crying, although I have learned to see the lessons in it.

I once again have a sense of humor about life. One of my email signatures is "I came here to find myself. I didn't like what I found. I'm going back." (I know I am the only one who really gets the joke since what I am going back to is the good, not the sorry excuse for a life that I created.) Another is "Manic Depression has given me the ability to do great things in my life, or at least the delusion to think they were!". "If you think my mood is unbearable to you, just think how it is for me." I think it is important to have a sense of humor. The challenge is hard enough as it is.

I know I painted a pretty ugly picture of myself and it is all too true. I am very uncomfortable about it and embarrassed to tell anyone, especially so publicly as in a book. I hope you can accept me for having the courage to tell the truth and not try to hide the parts I am afraid you will judge me harshly for. I hope you can feel the sincerity in my attempt to improve. My goal is that you will join me in working on our interior lives together and inspiring others to look deeply inside theirs. If I help just one other person to improve this bipolar condition then my intention was good. If it helps me to improve myself, then I have truly made the world a better place.

How is your Interior Life?

Are these concepts new to you? Have they made you start to look within?

If bipolar is to be considered a disorder, it is a disorder of our interior lives. Sure, we mess up our exterior lives too, but it is, after all, an illness of the mind. Your interior life is where the illness exists and where it can be turned into an advantage.

The Bipolar Advantage is that we have no choice but to pay attention to our interior lives. Other people might go through a life of constant distractions, but we cannot afford to. Sooner or later we have to face the demons within and use our superior creativity to find a way to turn them to our advantage.

Introspection with acceptance of what you find is the only way to really know what your interior life is. Please commit to looking within on a regular basis and you will surely find it is the greatest thing you have ever done.

Part 2: A Successful Bipolar Lifestyle

I designed a one day version of the Bipolar In Order Workshop on the belief that it would be attractive to people who did not have the time or resources to do a two day event. I stopped at the end of Introspection, which is the end of the first day anyway, and just left out the entire second day. It didn't work nearly as well as the two day workshop. I went back to the two day format and it only got better since I now began to understand the importance of the second day.

Do not underestimate the importance of knowing the truth of who you really are. Few people even seek the truth. The Bhagavad Gita[1], one of the holiest books in the world, says that out of 1000 people only one wants to know his/her 'true' self, and only one out of 1000 of them actually do. That makes it only one out of a million people who are really true to themselves. We have the key to knowing our 'true' selves; introspection and the desire to love and accept ourselves. We also have the desire to make ourselves better. We are already

---

1 Bhagavad Gita is the Hindu equivalent of the Bible. The story is from 3102 B.C.

in the top .1% of the world! That makes us 'one in a thousand'.

How do we become 'one in a million'? First we have to realize that just knowing the schmuck that we are does not mean we know our 'real' self. Our 'real' self is deeper than that. Our 'real' self is the perfect saint that is hidden behind all of our bad traits like the core of an onion is covered up with layer upon layer of shell. Our 'real' self is quietly waiting for us to peel back those layers and finally know who we really are - the perfect human. And for that it takes more than just acceptance and introspection. It takes changing ourselves into a better and better person until all of the layers of garbage are removed.

What is it that we need to remove? You know what your bad traits are, or at least will know as you become more aware of your 'true' self. Acceptance will let you admit them and introspection will help you to root out their every occurrence. But then you come up against the worst adversary of all, your habits.

Habits Control Your Life

Did you ever do something over and over that you know you shouldn't do? Do you brush your teeth twice a day? Did you ever keep repeating the same song in your head over and over again? Do you tend to wake up the same time every day no matter what time you go to bed? Do you know how to tie your shoes? All of these things are the results of habits, both good and bad. Can you tell which are the good and which are the bad habits? Not this list. ALL of your habits.

We couldn't live without the power of habits. Habits make it so we don't have to consciously figure it out every time we do something. Subconscious habits help us to breathe. Our heart has a habit of beating to keep our blood flowing. Our grooming habits keep us presentable so we can get close enough to people to chase them away with our bad habits. Our entire life is controlled by our habits.

How habits work

A habit is the result of repetition. Every time we repeat a thought or action, the tendency to repeat it again is made stronger. Every time we practice a golf swing or a basketball free throw, we are reinforcing a habit to work to our advantage. When we were born, we started to develop the habits that keep us alive. We learned how to breathe, to eat, to speak, to walk, to manipulate our parents, and to live in society. Each habit started with the first action followed by repetition until it became automatic.

A habit is neither good nor evil. It is simply the tendency to repeat a thought or action. Some habits are so strong because we could not live without them. Some, like smoking, are so strong that we can't live much longer with them. All habits get stronger every time we repeat them. Eventually we lose all choice and the habit runs automatically every time the trigger sets it off.

A habit itself is just an automatic response. It has no value. The decision of good or bad is made by us and is dependent on our values. A great golf swing habit is valued by Tiger Woods and hated by many wives around the world whose husbands are too busy playing golf to pay attention to them. The habit to have sex is what keeps every living thing alive but is considered horrible by many of the human species. We need to sort out for ourselves whether a habit is one we should develop or one to avoid.

Once a habit is fully developed, it is almost impossible to stop. The habit of living is so strong that even those of us who are expert at breaking it (we bipolars) fail on most attempts. Habits can be broken, but the effort involved can be enormous. It is way easier to never develop the habit in the first place if it is one you do not value. It is also easier to break a habit the moment you notice it is taking over than to go on repeating it until it is too late. In many cases just one repetition is enough to bring you past the point of no return. That is why groups like Alcoholics Anonymous feel that you should never repeat the drinking habit even one time if it has you in it's clutches.

Choosing the right habits

We choose which habits we develop by simply repeating them. Each repetition is like a vote for the habit and against all of the other choices we could make. There are only so many hours in the day, so whatever habits we vote on the most get to rule the democracy of our internal lives. Without tremendous lobbying, the new habit doesn't stand a chance against the ingrained habits who were voted into office so many times. The bad habits will fight to the death to keep their place of power. That is why it is so important to cast every vote wisely.

Trouble is, the bad habits are so much more fun. There is so much short term reward in choosing wrong that the odds are stacked against us. By the time we are old enough or wise enough to know the long term consequences of our short term pleasures, it is too late. People try to warn us. We blow them off like they don't know anything or are too hung up on their overblown morals. We think that there is no problem enjoying the forbidden fruit because we can always stop if it starts to be a problem. "One more time won't hurt." "I can stop after that." "I need it." "I'm bored." "It helps take the pain away." We have so many excuses because the habit does not want to lose its power. Just like our politicians, our bad habits will lie to us and do anything to hold on to the power we voted them into.

How do we get into some of the worst habits? First time I smoked a cigarette I choked. I hated it. Everyone said it was cool. I decided I was cool enough without it. I tried pot. I liked it. I got lucky and stopped liking it so much and it got outvoted after winning tons of elections. I tried masturbation. I liked it. A lot. It got elected president. Found out about other ways to get off. They were fun too. Kept voting....

Bad habits are against us

But why would people keep voting for things that bring them pain? Like cutting themselves. I don't know. I don't do that one. But I know a lot of people that do and they tell me it brings them into the moment. It is so intense that all other pain goes away. For the moment that they are cutting it must be true. Same affect can be had from meditation. I know that one. Voted for it more than any other. I also know that it takes so much effort to keep up that I understand why someone would vote for a method with more immediate rewards.

Whoever set this democracy up was a sadist. The things that are good for us not only produce less immediate rewards, the votes for them don't count as much. The ones that are the worst get ten votes for every one. We are set up to fail. The reward for the saint is that he gets to know that he is doing the right thing. The reward of the sinner is a life of fun. Our society currently votes for the sinner, too. The business man who runs a company like Enron gets to screw everybody, and the reward is a life of luxury, power, health insurance, better schools for his children, etc. The saint gets ridiculed and called a fraud for trying to be a better person.

Bottom line is everybody in the world has the deck stacked against her and the bipolars get nothing but jokers and wild cards. Unless our education system starts teaching the concepts of introspection, acceptance, and habits at an early age, our habits will control our lives. We foolishly take up so many habits without realizing the power they will have over us. By the time we wake up, it is almost too late to change them.

Changing our habits

So how do we change our habits? It is very hard to do and to claim otherwise is just lying to ourselves again. People say "just pick a good habit to replace the bad habit with." Not so easy for several reasons; the bad habit has the advantage of being more fun, it has accumulated a lot of votes, and it now earns 100 votes to one on each repetition. Sometimes you are better off picking a less bad habit to run against it until you defeat it. Then you can whittle down the base of voters until that new bad habit has not had time to accumulate power. It is better to use discrimination and realize that some things are just too dangerous in the long run to start up in the first place.

Another winning strategy is to attack the weak habits first until you build up the willpower to go after the really pernicious ones. You can never win against all of them at the same time, but you might be able to pick off the easy targets while building up the strength of the good habits for later battles. As they say in war and marriage; you have to pick your battles. Every win helps you to gain strength for the next battle. It pays to pick off the easy targets first. This is what they mean when they say to go for the low hanging fruit.

Don't be discouraged. It is really hard to find out about our habits and to face the battles ahead. Just like when you first found out about being bipolar, facing your habits is a great first step toward winning the war and turning bipolar from a disorder into an advantage.

Where is the advantage to being bipolar? Perhaps in our suffering we have been made aware of the need to change our habits. Those who can comfortably ignore their bad habits will wake up in their old age and realize they made the wrong choices all along. I saw it myself when I was 28 and ran a retirement home. It was such a great lesson for me to see the results of people's choices and the huge difference in the lives of those who chose wisely. Too bad it took me so long to heed the lessons I was fortunate to discover early in life.

Time to brainstorm again

What bad habits do you have that are weak enough for you to attack? Write down five if you can.

Look at your list and write down as many ideas as you can for how to beat them. Go over the list and make sure you are picking easy wins.

Which ONE are you going to put on your introspection list? Go do it now. Make sure you put it in the form of a question.

Congratulations! You are 'one in ten thousand' now. You are well on your way to being 'one in a million!'

Good Mental Habits

The mind is the most powerful force in the universe. It can create incredible cities, gorgeous cars for the roads, planes for the skies, and boats for the water. It can create beautiful music for the ears, art for the eyes, and stories to entertain itself forever. It can feel love, endure great pain, and attain states of bliss that few have been able to achieve. It can then wake up, forget the dream entirely, go flip burgers for minimum wage, come home to watch 'reality TV,' and find life fulfilling. Not my mind.

The 'normal' mind is equipped with a governor. It is protected from having the dreams merge with 'reality.' It can't feel the depths of despair so that the body kills it in desperation. It can't get too excited for fear that it might do something 'crazy.'

The bipolar mind is an entirely different thing. We get to experience the whole spectrum of emotions. Our imagination is so strong that we can dream while simultaneously being in the 'real' world. Bipolar people are way over-represented in the arts when compared to any other group[1]. We are well-represented in the ranks of the

---

1 Kay Jamison, *Touched with Fire*, page 88, Figure 3-3. New York, Free Press Paperbacks, 1994

genius, the inventors, the mystics, and the madmen. We are the explorers. Not content with the mundane, we set out to find new adventures and to turn our dreams into a reality that we can share with others. We are the lucky ones with a mind that has no limit.

Unfortunately, nobody ever taught us how to get our mind under control, so we suffer greatly. We can learn from those explorers who came before us and turn what was perceived as a curse into a Bipolar Advantage. We only need to be shown the way.

5,000 years ago, in what is now India, there was a culture that made exploring the mind their greatest mission. They turned understanding the interior workings of thoughts into a science. They invented the oldest and most complex language that still exists today. That language, Sanskrit, is so advanced that the mere sound of a word creates a corresponding feeling in the mind. They called their science 'Yoga,' and to this day those who explore its depths are rewarded with a personal understanding and control of every thought and action.

Ever since these ancient yogis explored the mind, scientists have been trying to figure out how it works. We have made great advancements in recent brain research that has proven many of the yogis' ideas. Brain/mind research that tries to integrate both ancient and modern knowledge of the mind has been very fascinating and has produced remarkable discoveries. One thing the experts all agree on is that the mind has far more power than we can imagine and there is an endless amount still to learn.

I believe that bipolar people have a special capacity to explore the mind. The tendencies that we struggle with have been reported in the greatest saints, artists, and thinkers of all time. Learning to harness those powers and to control their side effects can make the difference between a life of fascination and a meaningless life of pain.

Science has given us tools for that exploration that are very powerful and effective. I will share some of the simpler tools with you here. If you find them interesting there is a whole new and exciting world waiting for you.

Memory exercise

We were taught to memorize in school. The school's method is to take a list and repeat it until you can remember it long enough for the test. After that you are free to forget it, because you can do the same again in the future if you ever need to again. It is a boring and tedious method that does not even work very well. How can the education system be so stupid? Science has proven that there are way better methods for memorization. Why don't they teach us those methods? Sure they come up with rhymes sometimes, but the mind is way more powerful than that. It is actually easy and I will prove it to you.

Remember the left brain-right brain stuff? Turns out that our memory is perfect when we use the right brain to remember and pretty bad at using the left brain for memory. The right brain is the creative side, the part we bipolars have an advantage with. The right brain uses visual and musical memory and the left side is stuck with logic and words. That's why you can remember the words to songs so well and can remember faces, but not names. We just need to take advantage of that.

To show you how to improve your memory, consider the following table:

ONE	BUN
TWO	SHOE
THREE	TREE
FOUR	DOOR
FIVE	HIVE
SIX	STICKS
SEVEN	HEAVEN
EIGHT	GATE
NINE	WINE
TEN	HEN

Because each pair is a rhyme it is easier to remember. Try to remember it using the natural rhyme and rhythm of the items; one-bun, two-shoe, etc. How did you do? You don't need to right now, but if you like what we are about to explore you will need to commit the table to permanent memory. There is a whole science to permanent memory, but there is only so much space in one book.

The mind has perfect visual memory. The trick is to pair the number of the item you want to remember with the rhyming item. For example: One-bun and I want to remember a hot dog. I picture the hot dog in a bun - easy. O.K. Two-shoe and I want to remember ice cream. This one takes some imagination but we bipolars are great at that. Visualize a shoe smashing ice cream. Get the idea? Hot dog in a bun is not only a bad choice because you think it is obvious, but your right mind doesn't like it either. The right mind likes the picture to be memorable. That means wild and crazy. WE are wild and crazy. What a coincidence!

Let's try again. One-bun and the first item is chocolate sauce. Remember the sexy blonde in the grocery store? What do you mean you don't remember? Well she has great buns. Picture you got her home and proceeded to pour chocolate sauce on her buns. Did I mention that wild and crazy is great, but sex is fabulous? No seriously. If your image has sex in it you have an added ability to remember. Aren't bipolars perfect with our natural tendency for sexual promiscuity? And you thought that was a bad trait.

Now we have a sexy blonde with chocolate on her buns but she has cold feet because her shoes are made of ice cream. Do you think you can remember that one? Time for the test. What are the two items you wanted to remember? Too easy. Could have remembered them without all the fun, but this method works for a hundred items just as well.

Time for the real action. Pull out that grocery list we made before or brainstorm up a new one now. Better yet, make a real grocery list of ten items that you need and when finished with this exercise go to the store and get them. Take ten items and pair them up with the rhymes. Get out your bipolar creative mind and create bizarre images. You don't have to make one visualization with a blonde, barbecue sauce, razor blades, and laxatives. You can and should create ten separate visualizations, one for each item.

Did it work? Of course it did. I liked the one with angels spraying whipped cream to create the clouds in heaven. You didn't need to have them in their panties but it added a nice touch. Get it? Seven-heaven and the seventh item on the list is whipped cream? Would have worked good for remembering panties too, especially if you visualize those big white ones that come up almost to the belly button that old ladies like to wear. You know, the ones that you can partially see through the front and with fart stains in the back. You don't have to tell anyone what you visualize so have fun with it.

This is just a small taste of the power of the mind. With practice you can use this technique to remember everything. The guy who taught it to me was Frank Clement. Frank invented the touch screen computer and the speaker phone among many other things before founding the Boulder Center of Accelerative Learning. He built the 'Dynamic Accelerative Learning System' by putting together state of the art brain research gathered from all over the world. I helped facilitate his workshops for a couple of years. A group of us used to sit around and play with this technique to see how far it could go. Frank was the best. Fifteen of us would throw out any word we could think of in random order and he would take just one second to come up with a visualization and say he was ready for the next one. When we got to 150, he would instantly rattle off the list, pointing at who said each word. He would then do it backwards, forwards, and random.

There are many other techniques for memory that are very effective. If you like the idea do a search for memory techniques on the internet and have fun. It might not be earth shaking, but it helps me to make up for the ravaging effects of the lithium that I take. It is also a very good habit for stimulating your mind and can even be used against one of the bad habits by keeping your mind occupied with better things. I sure hope nobody mentions panties for the next few days.

Visualization

We talked about the power of visualization related to memory. It is even more powerful when used in other ways. Top athletes use visualization to get the competitive edge. Top business executives use it to create a strategy for the future. Inventors use it to solve complex problems. Writers use it to develop their stories. Artists use it to come up with their creations. Movie producers use it for everything. It's the 'vision thing' everybody talks about someone not having. And to think bipolar people have another major advantage in the visualization department. Are we lucky or what?

Before we can make any great thing happen in the 'real' world we have to first see it in our mind. Our mind is the perfect laboratory because through visualization we can see all sides of a design without having to build a model of it. We can combine visualization with brainstorming and solve the biggest problems known to man. We can see all of the colors and permutations until we come up with a form worth putting to paper. Once our idea takes 'real' shape we can let our subconscious mind take over and come up with improvements and solve the inevitable design problems. Whether aware of it or not, every great thing man has created had visualization as a central component in the process.

The link between visualization and the body is an amazing one. You can actually do exercises solely in the mind and they have a provable effect on your body. Top athletes use this to sharpen their skills without adding to the strain on their bodies caused by repeating the same motion too many times. And who hasn't visualized the perfect partner while stimulating his/her own body? Through visualization, you can learn to relax, take a mental vacation, or focus on winning the next tournament. Sports teams have been exploring this aspect of visualization for many years now and believe it is a strong component in training programs.

There are so many more aspects to visualization, but once again, that it is for another book. If you find this to be an interesting topic, you can find many articles and books on the internet to get started on another exciting new habit.

There are many different visualization exercises for every goal. What I want to share with you now is one that produces relaxation. You can practice it until you are very skilled at it and it will come through for you on one of those nights when you are too tense to fall asleep. I cannot read this to you while you lie down with your eyes closed, so you will just have to read over the instructions and make it up as you try it later.

Lie down in bed or on the floor where you can be comfortable. Cover yourself with a blanket if you need to. The important part is to find a relaxing position so you can start to forget about your body; we don't need it for this exercise.

Close your eyes and relax. Take a couple of deep breaths and when you let the second one out just forget about your breath altogether. Imagine yourself lying in the bottom of a rowboat floating down the river. It is a slow moving river and you can feel the gentle rocking of the boat as it drifts slowly along. You can hear the water against the sides of the boat. You can smell the water and the clean air. You can feel yourself relaxing without a care in the world. The sun is shining and you can feel the warmth on your face.

The boat softly runs ashore and you decide to get up and explore. You walk up the shore into the forest. You can smell the moisture in the air and hear the sounds of the birds. As you walk a little while you come to a clearing. It is covered with tall soft grass. This grass is unlike anything you have ever seen. It is a very light purple and has the texture of one of those velour blankets. You walk through the grass and you can feel the softness on your legs. You smell strawberries and peaches. You decide to lay down and it is so comfortable it feels like you are floating on the clouds.

As you lay there you begin to feel a warm glow in your chest. You start to feel a very peaceful state and a feeling of pure love. As that feeling gets stronger so does the warm glow. It begins to spread throughout your body and it relaxes every part as it goes. The glow even starts to be the only thing you feel as your body starts to just disappear into it.

The only thing you can feel now is love and peace, and the warm glow. As it expands further, you feel it is taking up the whole clearing. It expands more and spreads across the forest and past the boat. With every pulse of the glow it gets bigger and the love gets stronger. Eventually it gets so big it covers the whole planet. It expands further and surrounds the sun and all of the planets. As it keeps expanding, it spreads across the whole universe. You are that whole universe of love now and the peace is remarkable. Just stay there for a while until you feel it is time to go. If you have not fallen asleep you can feel the glow contract all the way back down to your body until you feel yourself again. Try to hold on to that peace and love for as long as you can.

You can, of course, make up any visualization you want. To take yourself deep it helps to include all of your senses and imagine something that will help you become calm. Visualizing a dance club might help with your dance moves, but it certainly will not help you go to sleep.

There are countless worlds to explore in our minds. Properly directed, visualization can have tremendous results. Bipolar people usually have no problem doing it. Many of us visualize things even when we are fully awake in the world. Most of us don't like it because we are afraid of it and it distracts us. Some of us choose to daydream our lives away. Others come up with their best ideas by daydreaming. It is up to you to hone this ability into an advantage for you. Getting into the habit of practicing visualization can be a great habit to use against your bad habits.

Can you think of a visualization that might be fun for you? Can you think of a time when you might use this skill to solve a problem or practice a physical movement? Do you think this is just crazy and want to just put the book down? Whatever you choose, it is important to explore possible options that might help you to replace your bad habits with good ones. Visualization works great for me and many other people. You should at least give it a try.

Meditation

Meditation is the greatest action ever devised by man. Called by many names, it is the central practice of every religion in the world. Meditation is used by athletes and businessmen to improve focus, by parents to relax while raising teenagers, and by sex advocates to improve intensity and staying power. Every person in the world can practice meditation and it will make a difference in all who do it. The power of meditation cannot be overestimated.

Meditation is usually associated with religion. In the strictest definition, meditation means to focus 100% of your mind on God to the point of merging your consciousness with God's consciousness, also known as oneness with God. This state of merging is called Nirvana by the Buddhists, Ecstasy by the Christians, Samadhi by the Hindus, Illumination by the Jews, and Tabattal by the Muslims. Kids take a drug called Ecstasy, go to a club called Samadhi, listen to a band called Nirvana or music called Trance, and talk about how it makes them feel more connected. I think they are searching for the same thing and don't know the best techniques yet.

The practice of meditation is called various names too. It also goes by concentration, contemplation, prayer, focusing, quieting the mind, stilling the heart, communing with God, practicing the presence, feeling the peace, being in the moment, and more. It is all about taking the mind, that naturally goes out in every direction, and focusing it on one thing.

Focusing the mind can be compared to focusing light. If you take a 100 watt light bulb and put it in a pool of water it will light up the whole pool, but in the ocean it will only light up so deep. If you take the same 100 watts and focus it into a laser beam it will go right through to the bottom of the ocean. Same with the mind. If the mind is scattered in every direction it will barely see, but focused it can cut through to the depths of whatever you point it at. The key to success at anything is the ability to focus your mind on the subject at hand whether it is sport activity, business, study, religion, or controlling the bipolar mind.

The feeling of deep meditation is beyond compare. The Bible calls it a peace which "passeth all understanding[1]." It is the ultimate joy, the highest high, the greatest love, the deepest peace, the greatest happiness, and the most intense awareness you will ever feel. There is nothing else in the world that even comes one tenth the way there.

Everything we do is an effort to find happiness, joy, etc., but in the long run the efforts do not get us there. The new car (or clothes, toy, or whatever material thing we get) gives us a little pleasure, but after a while the joy turns into the pain of maintaining it and we need a new one.

---

1 Philippians 4:7

Meditation is the joy that just keeps on giving. The feeling of meditation is eternal. The mind never tires of true deep meditation. There is no better state to be in.

Then why, when you try to meditate, is it just frustrating and your mind wanders all over the place? Because it is the hardest thing you will ever do. The mind, and way more so the bipolar mind, wants to go all over the place. If it didn't, we would be so focused on reaching for the fruit that a tiger would walk up and eat us. We have a lifetime of the habit of an unfocused mind and it wants to be out of control. It is the reason most people don't meditate.

It takes so much effort to get the mind to focus just a little that we take drugs instead, imagining we are taking a shortcut. All that accomplishes is a high that is not even one hundredth of the high achievable via meditation, and it convinces the mind that it needs that new drug habit to get there. However, it only makes it harder to meditate. So you sit down to try and the mind fights back. Meditation is the greatest challenge you will ever face.

They call it 'practicing' meditation for a good reason. Technically you are not meditating until you are actually in the state of oneness with God. You are only practicing a technique that you think might help you to attain it some day. Nonetheless, so many people call any attempt 'meditation' that it is generally considered 'meditation' no matter what the effort. I go along with that while keeping the distinction that 'real' meditation is only when you are 'in the state' of meditation. The distinction is important because it reminds us that our efforts actually have a goal that is achievable and worth the effort. Most people are willing to settle on a definition of meditation that has a goal of relaxing just a little. I'm not. Don't you either.

Enough bullshit, how do you do it? There are as many techniques as there are people in the world. We all try something to quiet the mind and have varying degrees of success. Is it meditating to drink a beer and veg in front of the TV? If the goal is to take your mind off work and relax, in a way it is. It might be a crummy method for me, but if it works for you it might be better than the alternative until you create a better habit. On a scale of one to ten, the 'veg-and-beer technique' might only be a one, but the ten rated technique is too hard for most people to do. What you need is the method that works for you and is easy enough for you to keep practicing.

Once you develop the habit of meditation you can take on higher and higher techniques until you reach the ultimate goal. I can't imagine the 'veg-and-beer technique' getting you very far, but who knows? Saint Ignatius used the 'horse hair shirt and torture yourself' technique and it worked for him[1]. Joan of Arc used the favorite bipolar technique of going into a rage and slashing up the enemy[2]. Everyone thinks that his is the best technique and tries to push it on everyone else. The best technique is what is best for a particular person at that point in time, so don't fall for it. My technique is the best and you should do it my way :-). Just kidding.

---

1 Christian saints have to hold the record for weird ways of achieving oneness with God. Suffering as a path to greatness is not my favorite by any means. The Hindus are the bunch I relate to. Even sex fits in for them as a legitimate form of meditation.

2 "The Messenger: The story of Joan of Arc" Directed by Luc Besson, Starring Milla Jovovich, Columbia Tri-Star, 1999

I started at 5 years old watching my breath as a meditation technique and it worked great for me. Still does. Whenever I stop meditating because of going too manic or depressed, I always return to that simple technique again for a while before taking up other ones. If it works for you, great. If not, try another one. Like I said, there are as many techniques as there are people. There is no best technique no matter how many times I tell you mine is the one.

Sit in a comfortable position or lay down. Just like in visualization you need to get rid of the body because it causes too many distractions until you are REALLY good at meditating. Some people like to do walking meditations and they work great for them, but it is easier at first to forget the body. Unlike the visualization, you do NOT want your mind to wander. You want it to focus on one thing and ONE THING ONLY. The breath is not only a convenient thing to focus on, it also gives feedback at the same time by slowing down as you go deeper.

Watch your breath come in and watch it go out. Just make a note of it, don't try to control it at all. Your mind will instantly go off to some other thought and when you catch it (sometimes ten minutes later) just go back to watching your breath. Do not judge yourself for failing or force anything, just calmly go back to watching your breath. The more you practice, the longer you can keep watching without distraction. At first it will be a few seconds, but eventually you can go a whole minute without another thought. For that minute nothing else exists, only the breath.

Eventually, as you become calmer, you start to notice that your breath slows down a little. You are starting to get there. Just notice it and keep watching. If you try to force it by controlling your breath you are making a mistake. Just watch the breath as if you are watching somebody else. The slower the breath gets the more relaxed you become. The more relaxed you become the more you start to lose focus again and the mind drifts away. It happens to everyone, so don't be hard on yourself. Just remember to go back to watching your breath every time you catch your mind doing something else.

Try this exercise for three minutes every day and when you are comfortable go to five. Keep adding to the length of time you practice until you find it is too hard to keep up the habit. Back off until you find a length of time that you can stick with every day. There is no advantage to doing this for a long period if it breaks your habit. This is not a competition that the winner is the one who can go the longest. The winner of the time game always loses out to the winner of the deep game. It is incomparably better to go very deep for ten seconds than to do a shallow effort for eight hours a day as some people do.

Meditation is a life-long pursuit. It is not a race to the finish line. It takes time to get to the deeper states, and there are no shortcuts other than better techniques that you cannot try until you have developed strength of focus. The technique I just outlined will get you there and you do not need any other technique, although for variety it is fun to try them. At first you feel momentary glimpses of peace and they start to become both deeper and longer-lasting. You also learn to go deep much faster, so even a brief effort can return you to a deep meditative state. As that happens, the effect starts to spill over into your daily life even when you are not meditating.

After much time and practice, your breath starts to slow so much that you notice that the pause between the out and the in breath starts to expand. It starts to take a second between, then a few seconds, and eventually a minute passes between the time you breathe out and the time you take another breath. You are not holding your breath. That ruins everything and will never work. You are just observing and making note of the feedback. After a while you stop even making note of it since it happens a lot and it is no big deal. It never was a big deal. The big deal is that along with the pause comes that state of such profound peace that I mentioned earlier. In time, the breathless state gets longer and the feeling of peace gets deeper. The experts at it have such control that they can achieve that state instantly and stay in it for a really long time.

I remember a long time ago I was at a lecture on meditation and the woman on stage was the most advanced at it I have ever met. After the lecture she suggested we try. I was close enough to her to see her breathing. She took one breath, let it out, and didn't breath again for ten minutes. A friend who was running the microphone pinned to her chest said he could hear her heart stop. When she came back she said, "if you could just feel it for one second it would change your life forever." It did not matter if I saw her breathe, everyone in the audience said later that they could feel a wave of peace take them over like they had never felt before.

Her teacher was in that state even while talking, eating, running, and in everything he did. He no longer had to practice because he was in that state all of the time. According to the Bhagavad Gita, he was one of those who actually knew his true self, a 'one in a million.' I find it very exciting that the world has so many millions that don't even care to look for the state, that I can be a 'one in a million' too.

Being bipolar is not an advantage in meditation unless you think it's an advantage to have a harder time of it. Our bipolar advantage of having a mind that goes off in every direction makes it so much harder to do. The advantage we gain from even the weakest effort of meditation is in the fact that we learn to get the monkey of our mind under control. That alone makes it the most important treatment we could possibly do. If there is just one thing from this book you take with you it should be introspection. If you take up a second habit please give meditation a try. It may turn out that being bipolar is the best thing that ever happened to you for the sole reason that it frustrated you enough to start meditating and stick with it.

Learning

The mind needs stimulation. If we don't exercise our mind it weakens just like our body does. It is bad enough that the drugs we take dull our minds; we don't have to add to the problem by lack of exercise. Learning makes our mind active, it gives us something to think about, and it helps us to learn tools to use in the battle against our condition. Learning is an important habit for keeping our mind in the best shape we can.

The topic really doesn't matter. What IS important is that we are interested in the topic enough to get enjoyment out of it. Learning about bipolar might not be fun, but the more we know about it the better we are in accepting it and doing something about it. I choose to learn as much about bipolar as I can, while entertaining my mind with other topics. I read everything. For me it is absorbing information and I have a ravenous appetite. I pick up whatever is in front of me and read it no matter what the topic.

There are so many sources of information to explore about bipolar. Books are a good place to start, but most of them are dry and boring, or focused on the negative. That is why I am writing this one. There is also a ton of information on the internet, just be careful to question the source and consider it carefully. You also need to narrow your search. A Google search on 'bipolar sex comedy' turns up 224,000 pages.

Support groups are a great resource. Finding other people who have the same or similar experiences can literally be a life saving discovery. Sure, lots of them are idiots who just talk about what they had for lunch and how their life sucks, but I go just the same. I have learned great things from the 'what I had for lunch' crowd. Just because someone might not have my I.Q. doesn't mean they can't make brilliant observations that I could miss in my arrogance.

Support groups have probably taught me the most about bipolar. With proper guidance, they can bring up topics that are never discussed with doctors, therapists, clergy, parents, loved ones, and 'normal' friends. Support groups are one of the best places to learn more about bipolar. There is one warning though. Do you remember the story about the first meeting for me? Sometimes, and maybe even most times, the groups tend to be the 'what I had for lunch' and 'life sucks' crowd. If you find one like that, feel free to walk out at any time. Please look for another one though, because meeting other people who share our condition can make a huge difference.

It may seem that I am anti doctors and anti drugs, but nothing could be further from the truth. I complain because doctors do not have the perfect solution and the drugs have side effects I don't like. I have seen so many cases where people are still alive today and living much better lives because of the medical community. Your doctor and therapist can be the best resource you have and the difference between a life of hell and one that works. They are the experts who have dedicated their lives to helping and have studied way more than I am willing to do. They also see our stuff all day long five days a week. You deserve a good doctor and expert care. Make sure you find it, because you will need it.

The trouble with doctors is you. You need to change the way you look at them. You are not a child who needs mommy to make all of your decisions, but that is the way you may look to your doctor. My doctor might have studied more than me and knows the statistics better than I do, but I know myself better than he ever will. I treat him as an equal and demand that he treats me the same. He likes it that I am an active participant in my mental health and he is a great resource not only for drugs, but for insight and advice. If he suggests that I try a new medication I make him tell me a brief overview about it including dosage parameters and all. I agree to stay on the dose only if I make the final decision and I promise to comply fully once I agree. I then research the drug and might even ask his opinion on others that are comparable. He gives me a great argument as to why he thinks this is the right course of action or else I do not follow it. He knows I am serious and he does not have to worry about compliance. The doctor/patient relationship can be a great resource - use it.

Memory exercises, visualization, meditation, and learning will all contribute to your 'brain therapy.' They will all help in keeping your mind tuned up and in focus. Introspection is probably the most effective tool for learning about your condition. Please give introspection a try if you haven't already.

Good Physical Habits

Having your body fall apart will only make it harder to handle bipolar. It is hard enough to battle your mind, you don't want to make it harder by neglecting your body. Keeping up good physical habits will make a huge difference. Being in great shape can be the difference between a depression that puts you out of action and one that only slows you down. Being in good shape might help you to survive the stress of a manic episode too.

There are four main areas to consider in taking care of your body in addition to good nutrition. Optimal physical fitness is only achieved by combining all four types of exercise with a diet that supports you well. The four types are; strength, endurance, flexibility, and relaxation. Strength is best developed with resistive weight training. Endurance is developed via aerobic exercise. Flexibility comes through stretching. Relaxation is helped greatly via orgasm, but we can't talk about that here. Good nutrition, of course, is best achieved through proper eating, but you already knew that.

Resistive weight training

In 1996 the Surgeon General of the United States said that resistive weight training was one of the most important things the elderly can do for their health and it was a breakthrough in elder care[1]. In 1994, Joycelyn Elders, The Surgeon General of the United States, said that masturbation would help in the fight against AIDS and got thrown out of office the next day by Bill Clinton[2]. What's up with that? Talk about hypocrisy. But sex is for a later chapter. You can flip forward if you need to. Just seeing if you were paying attention.

Have you ever hurt yourself while lifting something that was too heavy? Of course you have. We have all made that mistake at least once in our life. Have you ever been embarrassed and uncomfortable going to the beach because your body looks bad? I have. Did you ever have to call somebody over to lift something and they made it look easy? All of these problems and more can be solved with resistive weight training.

Strength training is important for all of us no matter what our age. Unfortunately, it was never taught to anyone other than those who got lucky enough to find a good trainer at the gym. I spent a lot of my life at the gym, and I assure you that finding a good trainer is like finding a politician who doesn't lie.

You need good information to do strength training properly, and I am not going to give it to you. There is not

---

1 U.S. Department of Health and Human Services. Physical Activity and Health: A Report of the Surgeon General. Atlanta, GA: U.S. Department of Health and Human Services, Centers for Disease Control and Prevention, National Center for Chronic Disease Prevention and Health Promotion, 1996.

2 http://www.jackinworld.com/library/articles/elders.html

enough space. All I can do here is point you in the right direction.

The most basic principle is that your muscles get stronger if made to work and get weaker if allowed to remain at rest all the time. Nutrition has a role, but we will cover that in the nutrition section. If you put your arm in a cast because you broke a bone, your muscles will atrophy by the time your bone is healed. You will have to do therapy to restore your strength and that therapy will be resistive weight training. On the other hand, if you properly stress your muscles, they will grow bigger and stronger.

Of course you can't train your right arm and not your left or you will be unbalanced. But look at how many guys at the beach have huge arms and chest and toothpick legs. It is crucial that you train your body in balance. A strong abdomen and a weak back is a recipe for injury. This takes knowledge way past what I am going to cover here, so find a good book and read it.

Once you understand the importance of balance, it is time to start training. Most people waste their time and energy in the gym. Spending half an hour, three days a week, you can achieve the same results as someone who seems to live at the gym. This is because there is a science as to how often and how intense the exercises should be. Most people train too often so that their bodies do not have a chance to grow, and their training is not intense enough to create the stress necessary to stimulate growth. Again, it takes a whole book to cover this in the detail that you will need to be successful.

O.K. So where is this good book for me to read? "Body for Life" by Bill Phillips is a great place to start. I learned so much from Bill that I became a good enough body builder to be a male stripper. I worked out in half the time it took the other guys, and left the stage with twice the dollars. Bill Phillips is a genius about the science behind it all and can take you as far as you want to go both by providing physical regimens and by sharing the latest research.

Whatever you do, start out easy. Weight training is not a sprint. It takes a few months to get good results and if you hurt yourself in the first week you will never turn it into the great habit it should be. Begin with a low amount of weight and increase as you get more comfortable. Once you get used to the basics of weight training you will need to lift with full intensity. Anything less makes you spend too much time chasing the results you are after because you need to stimulate your muscles properly for optimal effect.

What does weight training have to do with the bipolar mind? Done properly, it demands 100% concentration. It has the same effect as meditation when it comes to training your mind to focus. This does not make weight training a replacement for meditation. It just helps by moving your mind in the same direction towards 100% focus. Remember, I said "done properly." That means exercising with such intensity that if the mind wanders at all you cannot accomplish the next lift.

Pumping iron isn't just for developing sexy pecs or a toned tush (although these are certainly motivating factors). The National Strength and Conditioning Association notes these additional benefits that you may enjoy as a result of weight training:

1. Resistance training may enhance cardiovascular health by mitigating several of the risk factors associated with cardiovascular disease by producing such changes as
    a. decreases in resting blood pressure, particularly in individuals with elevated pressures;
    b. decreases in exercise heart rate, blood pressure, and rate pressure product at a standard workload;
    c. modest improvements in the blood lipid profile;
    d. improvements in glucose tolerance and decreases in hemoglobin Alc in patients with diabetes mellitus.

2. Resistance training may result in improvements in body composition by maintaining or increasing lean body mass and producing modest decreases in the relative percentage of body fat.

3. Resistance training can produce increases in bone mineral density and may help delay or prevent the development of osteoporosis by reducing the age-associated loss of bone mineral density.

4. Resistance training may reduce anxiety and depression and may result in improved self-efficacy and overall psychological well being.

5. Resistance training can reduce the risk of injury during participation in other sports and activities. When performed correctly and properly supervised, it is in itself a safe activity with low injury rates.

6. Resistance training increases muscular strength and endurance, resulting in an increased ability to perform activities of daily living, and reduces

demands on musculoskeletal, cardiovascular, and metabolic systems.[1]

Aerobics

Aerobics is easy. Get out of bed, get moving, and get your heart rate up. Or you could just stay in bed, get a partner, and get it on. It really doesn't matter how you do it. Just do it!

There is only one objective with aerobics, to raise your heart rate to a target number of beats per minute. In the process, it accomplishes many other things, but the primary target is the heart. All you have to do is figure out your target heart rate and go. Of course, I am no doctor and am not giving medical advice. You should talk to your doctor before embarking on any exercise regimen.

To figure out your target heart rate, start with your predicted maximum. This is simple. Just take 220 minus your age. So, if you are 40, this calculation gives 180 is the predicted maximum beats per minute. You can then calculate the target heart rate from this predicted maximum, depending on what you are looking to accomplish.

• For warm-up, 50% to 60% is a good range for several minutes.

• For fat burning, 60% to 70% is a good range.

_____

1 http://www.nsca-lift.org/Publications/posstatements.shtml

• 70% to 80% puts you in the aerobic zone, where the most efficient training takes place, if you are fit enough to handle that intensity.

• 80% to 90% puts you in an anaerobic state where your body is not getting enough oxygen to maintain the exertion. Although there are some benefits from being in that range for a short while, it is hard to train efficiently at such a high intensity.

• 90% to 100% is the danger zone, and only people in very good condition should even attempt to go that far into the heart rate zone.

For a 40 year old who is in pretty good shape, the target range for the most efficient training is between 126 (180 x 70%) and 144 (180 x 80%).

How you get there is entirely up to you. There is no magic method that is better than any other. The best method for you is one that you will do on a regular basis at least three days per week. You also do not have to do the same exercise every time. You can dance one day, hike the next, bike ride two days later, and have sex the day after that. As long as the exercise puts you in the heart rate zone you are aiming for, you will get the benefit of aerobic exercise.

One other thing to consider is that you want to maintain the heart rate for 30 to 60 minutes. That means a fairly long walk or pretty good sex, you decide. Don't forget to warm up at 50% to 60% (90 - 108 for a 40 year old) for five minutes first and gradually build up to the target range.

My favorite form of aerobics is dancing. The music, the lights, the bodies, and the freedom to dance any way I want; it is a great way to enjoy my exercise. Of course, I am not talking ballroom dancing. I go to clubs that play trance, techno, house, club, and other forms of dance music that is high energy and fun. Just don't get so distracted by the thongs that you forget to dance. Gawking does not raise your heart rate enough unless there is something seriously wrong with you.

Contrary to popular opinion, aerobics is not the best way to get rid of fat. Strength training coupled with nutrition has that prize by a long shot. As an athlete gets in better aerobic shape, he actually becomes so efficient at burning energy that he burns a lot during exercise, but less than normal the rest of the day, and they cancel each other out. The stresses to the muscles caused by strength training take at least 48 hours to be repaired by the body and it burns calories at an accelerated rate 24 hours a day until repaired. Body builders have the lowest percent of body fat in the world.

There are tons of books and websites on aerobics. The Bill Phillips book you already bought for strength training will cover more than enough aerobics, too.

Aerobics also has a great effect on the mind. You must have heard of the runner's high. This is because the body produces endorphins that put you in a better mood. A good aerobics habit can make the difference between stability and slipping into depression.

Stretching

Are you Tense? Tight? Stressed? Strained? Uptight? Jittery? Twitchy? Squirrelly? In A State? A Bundle Of

Nerves? Under Pressure? Agitated? Fretful? Uneasy? Restless? Strung Out? Worked Up? Wound Up? Jumpy? Stomach In Knots? Worried? Panicky? Rigid? Stiff? Why do so many of these phrases for a state of mind use words that are more related to the body?

The body holds our tension and builds up to a point that it physically hurts. People say we need to relax, but the tension in the body often stays even when we relax the mind. Physical and mental tension are certainly connected, but I will cover the differences separately. We will look at stretching in this section and relaxation in the next.

As our muscles get tighter they put a tremendous strain on our bodies and minds. The wrong thoughts make our muscles tight. Weight lifting and aerobics do, too. The tension builds to the point in some people that it literally kills them from a heart attack caused by the heart trying too hard to pump blood through such constricted passages.

The way to counteract muscle tightness is stretching. Stretching should be a critical component in any exercise regime and for most people should be the first physical habit they take up. Stretching is also the easiest to do as well as the most pleasurable form of exercise, IF done properly.

First, we have to understand two extremely important concepts that most people neglect: balance, and not straining. Balance means you should take great care to stretch each side of the body the same; keeping it even. All good stretching programs have that already built in.

More importantly, and seldom mentioned, is the concept of not straining. The object of stretching the muscles is to relax the tension out of them, not to get them to stretch the farthest. Dancers go for the farthest stretch, but they are doing an athletic event and any athletic event taken to extremes is bad for you. Pushing yourself to the point of straining is counterproductive to your health and your ability to keep up the habit. You know you are straining too hard if you cannot hold a stretch for three minutes without it hurting so much you have to stop or back off.

Of course, you should once again ask your doctor if it is O.K. for you to start on any exercise regime. I'm not your doctor and don't pretend to be.

If it is O.K. with your doctor, you should try to sit on the floor with your legs straight out in front. Raise your arms above your head like you are reaching for the roof. Bend at the waist and see how close to your feet you can reach, keeping that reach the whole way down. Only go to the point of starting to feel a very slight pain. Try to hold it there while counting to 180, or set a timer for three minutes before you start. If you can hold for three minutes, you are doing fine. Your ego wants to know how far you go, so make a note of it. You will notice that if you do it the same time every day you will improve.

There is not enough room to go into a complete routine here, but just like with resistive weight training and aerobics, there are many fine books on the subject that will outline a good routine to follow. A book on hatha yoga is a great resource since hatha yoga is about the combination of stretching with meditation so you get double the benefit.

In addition to my meditation habit, if I were to take up only one more it would be stretching via hatha yoga. Don't forget introspection though. Introspection should be the foundation of all new habits because it is the way you know you are on track.

Relaxation

Relaxation means not doing or thinking about the things on your to-do list. Stretching may be relaxing and all, but it does take willpower to keep up the habit. By allowing yourself to just do nothing, you let your body heal and your mind relax without the strain of having to accomplish anything.

You can relax by just staying in bed and reading a book or even by sleeping. You can go to the beach, watch TV, listen to the radio, see a movie, have a great meal, or have sex. Anything that gives you a rest for a while is great. Just remember there is a fine line between staying in bed all day to relax and staying in bed for a month from depression. Introspection will help you to know the difference.

The important thing is that we all need time away from even our good habits. Sometimes the best habit is no habit at all. Make sure time to relax with nothing to do is part of your schedule.

Nutrition

I hope you have noticed by now that some foods affect your mood. What are they? Foods greatly affect your energy, too. Do you know what they are? We also need to know about how food affects our weight, especially because a lot of the drugs we take add to the problem. Our choice of food plays a much bigger role in our health than just giving us the pleasure of eating it. If you only eat foods that you like you will find out that the food does not like you.

Have you noticed what happens when you eat too much spicy food? Does it make you agitated? Or does it just make you feel warm and more energetic? How about sugar? Do you notice that an hour later you just want to take a nap? Haven't noticed? Good time to put a question in your introspection list. How about "Have I noticed how my mood changes when I eat spicy food?"

Richard Wurtman, M.D. and Judith Wurtman, Ph.D., scientists at the Massachusetts Institute of Technology (MIT), first linked food with mood when they found that the sugar and starch in carbohydrate foods boosted a powerful brain chemical called "serotonin." Soon they linked serotonin and other neurotransmitters (substances that pass information from cell to cell in the brain) to our every mood, emotion or craving. For instance, they noted that eating carbohydrate-rich foods (breads, cereals, pasta, fruits and starchy vegetables such as potatoes, winter squash or corn) elevated serotonin levels, helps you to feel more relaxed and calm; high protein foods (nonfat dairy products such as cottage cheese, yogurt or milk; or beans, peas, nuts and also soy products, such as tofu or soy milk) has the opposite effect: They release other substances that let you think and react more quickly, or feel more alert and energetic.[1]

Food affects our energy more than you know. Many people who have no energy are suffering from a bad diet and are looking for the doctor to diagnose an illness instead.

---

1 http://www.afpafitness.com/articles/FOODMOOD.HTM

What is often the real sickness is choosing foods that do not properly feed the body and mind.

The weight loss industry is making billions of dollars a year from something that should have been taught in high school. The concept is really very straightforward and makes perfect sense. If you eat more calories than you burn, you gain weight. If you eat less than you burn, you lose weight. So what's the big secret? Eat less and burn more calories if you want to lose weight. Or, if you are so addicted to food that you cannot control yourself, just burn more calories while introspecting on why you eat too much.

Have you heard of homeostasis? This is the concept that the body has a tendency to stay in the same state that it currently is in. Even if the current state of the body is bad, homeostasis is the tendency for it to stay that way unless influenced by outside forces.

Fighting against weight gain is very common for bipolar people. Many of the drugs we take for bipolar tend to make us fat. It is so common that you might mistake a bipolar support group meeting for an overweight support group or an Overeaters Anonymous meeting. The drugs we take for our bipolar condition take us out of homeostasis and make us gain weight. Removing this weight takes more than just a basic understanding of amount of calories taken in vs. amount of calories burned.

Homeostasis is what makes it more complicated for us. Once we put on the weight, it is very hard to get rid of it. If we lower our caloric intake, our body adapts to it in a very short time and lowers our metabolism to account for the lower intake of calories. Even if we exercise to make up for it, our bodies will burn muscle and save fat because they want to preserve fat levels to ward off starvation.

We have to trick our bodies if we really want to beat the fat problem. It is not that difficult once you understand the concept. If your body has a tendency to adapt to changes and hold on to fat, you just have to outsmart it. First off, if you eat less than 70% of your normal diet, the body freaks out and starts saving fat because it thinks it is starving. Secondly, if you eat 70% for three days in a row the body kicks into homeostasis and just lowers the amount it burns. You have to factor in both aspects to beat it.

The way to do it is to eat 70% of normal calories one day and 100% the next. But even that won't trick the body completely. As soon as it recognizes the pattern it adapts to it. What you have to do is get up in the morning and flip a coin. Heads is 100% of normal calories and tails is 70%. That way, it is random and the body can't adapt to it[1].

How do you figure out your 'normal' amount of calories? Just write down everything you eat for several days. Use a book or website that lists the calorie count of foods and total all the food you have eaten over those several days. Just divide it by the number of days and you have the average amount of calories per day. This number is the place to start as 'normal' for you.

You don't have to be fanatical about it. Just get a reasonable approximation of amount of calories and go from there. As long as you follow the rough plan outlined here, you will lose fat. Exercise like you always have (start

---

1 http://www.ediets.com/billphillips/diet/

exercising now if you don't), or increase the amount of your exercise to make even better gains. And don't forget to run this by your doctor before starting on any exercise or diet program.

Good Spiritual Habits

For so many people, the spiritual life is something they take up when the rest of their life falls apart. By then it is usually too late to develop the habits that would have helped them when times got tough. Without the stimulus of great loss, most people see little or no need to look to the spiritual life for answers. I was the opposite. I always knew I was different, it just took 45 years to figure out how much! I was fortunate to have developed great spiritual habits that got stronger in the good times and helped me to better survive the bad times.

One's spiritual life is an intensely personal thing. I am uncomfortable telling someone else what spiritual life to lead. All I can do here is try to highlight topics that I find important and share my own personal journey with you. Perhaps in doing that, it will inspire you to explore your own spiritual path more deeply.

Meditation

As I mentioned earlier, I have been fascinated with my breath ever since I was 5 years old. I intuitively knew that the relationship of breath to thoughts held the answer to life's great mysteries. I knew that there were people in every culture that were revered for knowing the 'truth.' These people were held up as the wise and noble spiritual leaders of society. I also knew that they all had found the secrets through the link of breath and mind and that I was destined to be one of them. Looking back, it seems that delusions of grandeur may have been the first sign that I was bipolar, but only ONE of the many signs I didn't recognize at the time.

The habit of deep contemplation or meditation is very strong in me. In spite of all the distractions and weird things I have done, the desire to meditate and to feel the direct experience of God were the greatest attractions of my life. How I managed to lead an intense spiritual life and still allow myself to stray so far from the principles I was trying to follow never made any sense until my diagnosis of bipolar. My justification prior to my diagnosis was that I was acting out the things that I knew sooner or later I would never do again. I was soon to be enlightened and would then spend the rest of my life as an ascetic holy man.

Sex, drugs, and every aspect of my life were always secondary to my desire to have greater and deeper spiritual experiences. I bent each act to include a spiritual component. Drugs were a way to deepen the experiences I was having in meditation, even if the setting was a dance club or hanging out with degenerates. Sex was a path to God that brought me to ecstatic states along with my partners, as was developed into a science in the Kama Sutra, written thousands of years ago. I now know that those excuses were actually slowing down my spiritual progress.

I always came back to meditation though. Now that the other things have less meaning to me, it is clear that I was very fortunate to have developed such a great habit. As

I said in the section on mental exercises, "Meditation is the greatest action ever devised by man." I hope you will at least give it a try.

Study

I was in my grade school library when I discovered that the rest of the world was not so interested in the life I was leading. I looked up everything I could find about religion, witchcraft, sorcery, shamanic rituals, and any topics related to the mind that I could find. As you can imagine, I found practically nothing. I knew that my search for 'the truth' was the highest path in every culture, and my direct experiences were as valid as those experienced by higher souls from every path. I also knew that this 'truth' was the same, although the paths taken to get there were extremely varied. Those paths and beliefs shared more common elements than differences.

In church, I was sure the banners proclaiming "God is Love," "Peace," "Joy," etc., were about the direct experiences I was having, and not the intolerance that the preacher was advocating. I was extremely attracted to the parts of the Bible that said, "the kingdom of God is within you[1]," or "Be still, and know that I am God.[2]" I know it is talking about the internal states I was experiencing. I fully understood how I could turn the other cheek because any other alternative would take me away from my direct experience of peace and joy.

---

1 Luke 17:21

2 Psalm 46:10

I was especially taken by the fact that for a brief moment on the cross, Jesus said, "My God, my God, why hast thou forsaken me?[1]" For that moment, Jesus had lost that direct experience I am speaking of; and, for me, it was reassuring that He could lose it and get it back to proclaim "forgive them, for they know not what they do.[2]" Perhaps there is hope for me.

I spent many hours studying the scriptures and every book I could find that talked about spiritual topics. To this day, I consider spiritual study one of the most important habits to develop. I worry, though, that without the foundation of a strong meditation habit, it is too easy to misinterpret what you are studying.

Fellowship

I spent countless hours visiting every church I could find. I mostly hung out at churches in silence, trying to feel the presence of God. Fervent prayer took place in those holy places, and it was easier to obtain the experience I was after because I could feel the peace that resulted from the efforts of others. Those visits convinced me of the correctness of my early beliefs; all religions are trying to obtain the same thing - direct personal experience of God, no matter what words they use to describe it. I always believed that all religions share 95% in common and kill each other over the 5% of differences that are not the central part of the truth anyway.

---

1 Mark 15:34

2 Luke 23:34

Sitting in the same space in silence for hours with someone has a remarkable effect. You become connected to that person in an amazing way. You can feel that she is on the exact same path as you, and an amazing fellowship exists without the need for words. Fellowship is another very important habit on the spiritual path, which is why churches exist in the first place. For me it didn't matter what the faith, I was a brother to those I met, even if we never spoke.

I talked with many of my spiritual brothers and sisters while sitting on the church steps after many hours of silence together. I could ask them any questions I wanted about their beliefs, and they never thought I was doing anything but trying to understand. I told them I was raised Christian, but believe we are all searching for the same thing. We had incredible conversations about the similarities of our beliefs and I learned so much about theirs. I strongly feel the world would be a much better place if we all look for the 'truth' in our similarities instead of our differences.

Reflection

Meditation, study, and fellowship leads to reflection. Even if you don't believe in a god, you have to admit there are questions to ponder. Why are we here? What is the meaning of life? What is the point of it all? Why do I have this awful mental illness? The habit of reflection helps us sort it all out. It gives meaning to an otherwise meaningless life. Even if your answer is "life sucks and then you die," we all have a need for reflection.

Introspection is a form of reflection. That is why the introspection chapter of this book includes spiritual matters.

Sometimes the only thing that keeps us from killing ourselves is the search for meaning that drives us to stay alive, even if just to find out why. Reflect on that one for a while.

Temptation

Find me someone who has not given in to temptation and I'll show you a liar and a hypocrite. Even Jesus gave in to the temptation to doubt during that brief moment on the cross. I bet you never thought of it that way before. If it was part of God's plan to have Jesus be the perfect example, what was the meaning of his moment of weakness? That is what acceptance is all about. We need to accept our failings while striving to be better people. In the Bible they call it forgiveness; same thing.

Just like everything else for me, 'if it's worth doing, it's worth overdoing'. I gave in to temptation with gusto. From my mid teens to my early thirties, I did more drugs, had more sex, and spent more time partying than most people without bipolar would do in ten lifetimes.

I also discovered Yoga. Yoga is not a religion. It is a set of practices that have the same effect no matter what your religious beliefs or affiliation. I did hatha yoga with the best of them. I twisted hatha yoga around the temptation to be an exhibitionist and did nude yoga in front of anyone who would watch. Nude yoga just so happens to be the fastest growing form of yoga today. I was ahead of my time again!

Hatha yoga is just a side show to the real thing, though. The real action in yoga is meditation and breathing, also known as pranayama. What a coincidence! The same things I have been into my whole life. And to think they built a science around these things five thousand years ago. This opened up a whole new spiritual life for me, and right in the middle of my years of giving in to temptation, I thought I was making the best spiritual progress. There's that delusion thing again!

My interest in yoga got me to explore, in depth, all of the great religions of the world. I studied with the Muslims, the Jews, the Buddhists, the Hindus, the Shaman, The Medicine Men, and I found them all so similar it was amazing. I started reading everything I could find from the brain and consciousness research community and discussed it with everyone I could find. My drug experiments became guided by the research into altered states of consciousness and took on a great spiritual meaning for me. My friends called me up and told me they made a movie about me called "Altered States." I took some LSD and went to it. Sure enough, it was a documentary of my life, including the delusions of the bipolar disorder that had not been diagnosed yet.

I go to the monastery

I was thirty, married, and had a 2 year old girl when my wife started claiming she was unhappy in the marriage. I agreed to go into counseling with her Lutheran minister to try to work things out. After the first half hour, the minister announced very smugly that they don't believe in monastic life, but if he ever met a monk, it was me. He suggested we divorce and I move to a monastery.

When we got home my wife said, "See, even the minister thinks we should divorce." I said "No way. We have a family and a responsibility that cannot be broken." She sued. I hung around waiting for the final divorce and then left for the monastery. Two months later, I found out from my ex-wife that the minister was kicked out of the church because he was married while having an affair with my wife and counseling me to leave. Have I mentioned I hate religious hypocrites?

Life in the monastery was the best part of my life. It was perfect. Everyone else was as obsessed with having a direct experience as I was, and I was finally accepted and acknowledged for what I was so good at. They called me Samadhi Tom because I was in a perpetual state of the heightened consciousness everyone was striving to achieve. I was so blissed out I thought the next breath was the one that was going to put me next to God for eternity.

Word came from home that my daughter Kate had abandonment issues and it tore me apart. Here I was, living my dream life, and driven into total depression by the guilt of what I was doing to my daughter. Kate and I have some kind of magical connection. We always have, and still do to this day. When Kate was born I looked right into the face of God. It was the most profound feeling of love I have ever had, and I still feel that way every time I see her.

I was still in bliss, but my energy was drained. They sent me to the doctor for tests every week and they could find no answers. I quit my habits for the first time in my life. I didn't have the energy or willpower to do the yoga. I couldn't meditate. I couldn't do anything but sleep all day. I became confused, despondent, and could hardly handle life at all. The senior monks invited me into their fold and I made the first commitment to becoming a permanent monk, but I could not keep it up. I finally left and drifted through a life without meaning for almost a year before being born again.

Back to the real world

You thought I was talking about born again like the Jesus freaks? Sorry, I was born again into sin. It was like starting all over, but I knew what to do this time. It had been four years since I had sex or drugs or any life outside of the straight-and-narrow, and I had some catching up to do. Besides I couldn't meditate, it was way too difficult.

Saint John of the Cross[1] talked about the 'dark night of the soul,' but I was not there yet. I wasted my next ten years living out my fantasies in a second childhood that went way beyond anything I had done before.

The Dark Night of the Soul

My real 'dark night of the soul' started with my diagnosis. I can't possibly explain it in a way you would really get the feel for it, but several months after my diagnosis I got a survey someone was doing to study the relationship that religion has with bipolar. My answers must have really shocked the guy, because he refuses to answer my emails. I hope you don't find them too offensive. After explaining my fervent spiritual life up to this point, I hope you can sense the intense darkness I feel and the confusion that I am still in right now. Remember that the questionnaire

---

1 www.catholicfirst.com/thefaith/catholicclassics/johnofthecross/dark_night/
darknight1.cfm

was a year ago, and I am on the way back. Please pray for my continued growth instead of wishing that I rot in Hell.

Sent: Sunday, September 05, 2004 10:53 AM

Subject: Re: bipolar and religion research

QUESTIONNAIRE

Male or Female:

male

Age:

48

Diagnosis:

Bipolar (Manic-Depression)

What is your religious tradition?

Born into Christian family, converted to Hindu-based church of all religions (Self Realization Fellowship) in early twenties. After diagnosis in 2002 am now agnostic at best, bordering on atheist.

Describe your understanding of God. (For those influenced by Buddhism and Hinduism, describe your understanding of the All-Encompassing.)

I currently have no understanding or belief in god. I used to think that God was the cause of everything like I am during my dreams. I never thought god was some guy sitting in the sky judging us, but more as a creator of some cosmic drama for his entertainment that needs us to go through the drama of life to keep the entertaining dream going.

If you consider yourself an atheist or agnostic, how has that (un)belief been influenced by your mental illness?

I had what I thought were direct experiences of God from an early age. These experiences included feeling an inner part of me separating itself from my body and floating above it as a silent witness, states in deep meditation of my breath and heart stopping and feeling an all encompassing love, feeling of connection to everything in the universe, and many more experiences. I nurtured and explored these experiences all my life and as I found the connection between my breath and the various states of mind, I started studying mind research and then religion to find an explanation. After various Yoga paths I came upon a teacher (Paramahansa Yogananda) who described these states exactly as I had experienced them and explained the relationship to breath and other techniques I had intuitively practiced from around 5 years old. I even ended up moving to one of his monasteries and pursuing it full time for about two years. After living with my diagnosis for 2 years, I now think it was all symptoms of my mental illness. In my explanation just now, I left out the phones that didn't ring when I heard them, hitchhikers on the road that were not there when I got closer, and many other strange visions and thoughts that definitely are mental illness.

How do you most experience God?

As a hate filled uncaring figment of imagination by fundamentalists of all faiths.

How do you least experience God?

As a loving being that actually cares about the humans that give him credit for being their all loving shepherd who watches over them.

How do you think your mental illness has strengthened your relationship with God?

I think it created and built up my entire relationship with God until I found out that it was all just a mental illness created delusion.

How do you think your mental illness has weakened your relationship with God?

It caused me to question the truth of my thoughts and perceptions, much less any imaginings of a God. I am not sure I actually did cry all day yesterday much less what happened the day before.

For bipolar disorder and other mood disorders, how would you describe yourself when you are manic/

hypomanic? Depressed? "Normal?" When do you like yourself the most?

When manic I love life and everybody loves me until I inevitably lose it and then everybody hates me and I feel guilty about my behavior. During those times when I am in a rage, I feel on top of the world and very high and invigorated by the thrill of the confrontation. I saw Zell Miller give his hate speech the other day at the Republican Convention (summer 2004) , and immediately thought "I know that state very well, perhaps as well as anyone in the world." There is so much more to say about it from so many perspectives, but suffice it to say that when I am manic, I am glad to be alive and have unbounded energy, I am extremely clear and fast thinking, and have a higher perception of everything and the delusion to think I am the only one who knows anything. I have been very successful in that state and have a resume to prove it.

When depressed the whole world is dark and I cannot remember any time that it was not or envision any time in the future that it might not be. The pain is unbearable. I cannot function and spend most of the day in bed or vegging out in front of my computer or the TV. My energy is gone and my thoughts are about death and pain.

When so called "normal" I don't have a lot of

energy either, but the world seems normal except for frequent visions of driving off a cliff or swerving into oncoming traffic. This has been going on my whole life and I thought it was normal until I was diagnosed and started asking other people who have the same disorder. Normal is also populated with frequent visions of things that are not there, or the formerly loved and now dreaded feeling that I am in a strange tunnel where time is slowed down and perceptions heightened to the detriment of normal perception of reality. I used to think those times were direct experience of God too.

How do you experience God differently when you're (for bipolar and other mood disorders) hypomanic/ manic? when you're "normal?" when you're depressed? (for schizophrenia) when experiencing mood changes, psychotic episodes, and other symptoms?

I have no experience of God at any time. What is "normal"?

If you never had another manic/hypomanic episode or depressive episode (for bipolar and other mood disorders) or severe psychotic changes (for schizophrenia), how would that affect your relationship with God?

At this point, if I never had another episode I would believe in miracles.

What religious stories (Judeo-Christian, Muslim, Buddhist, or other) have influenced your spiritual journey as a person living with a mental illness?

I have read most of the main ones from every faith, but only the Hindu stories make psychological sense to me because they are the ones who studied the psychology about the various states of mind for thousands of years. I always thought the fables made up by all of them were what was wrong about each of them.

The direct experience of the 'wise' or 'mystical' ones was the truth that they all had in common. I always thought that the proof was in that different cultures, uninfluenced by one another, came up with the same truths, so those truths are correct, and the different stories that put them in conflict with each other were where they are wrong.

How do you think your Holy Scriptures (Bible, Torah, Koran, etc) has addressed your mental illness?

Hindu scriptures describe states I have experienced in a clear, analytical way. The Bible is so much an analogy and parable that nobody can even agree on what it says. Same for the Koran, Torah, and others. They are more about a fable than about mental states. The Buddhists talk a lot about mental states too, but not to the level of detail worked out by the Hindus.

*From your perspective, have your Holy Scriptures
portrayed your mental illness in a positive or
negative way? Explain.*

I think many of the heros of the various faiths
were bipolar, including Joan of Arc and all the
others who had visions and acted in a way that
was totally different from the rest of society.
Those that were not exalted as saints were
burned at the stake, stoned, locked up, or
condemned to excommunication. Is possession
by the devil just an ignorant way of describing
manic-depression?

*Describe any biblical characters with whom you
identify as a result of your mental illness.*

Job and the description of hell just about covers
it.

*How has your faith helped you deal with your
mental illness?*

It makes it worse because it adds a major
conflict to the picture.

*Describe any spiritual disciplines you use and their
effectiveness.*

I have meditated almost my entire life. I know
that it makes so much difference that it is
amazing that I would not do it all the time.
Nonetheless, in many of my mental states for
the last ten years it is impossible to do and the
frustration of not doing what I clearly believe

in tears me apart. I have found it impossible so far to establish any consistent practice. I have direct experience over and over again that it makes me so much better, but just when the habit is being established and the positive effects are being felt, something distracts me from doing it and weeks go by before I try to take it up again.

Describe a story that typifies the relationship between your mental illness and your spiritual journey.

The movie called "The Messenger" pretty well describes it from her manic rages in battle to her doubts about her visions just before she was crucified by the church she believed in her entire life.

How do you think religious communities have understood and addressed your mental illness?

I think churches are a mental illness. How else can you account for the Christian right watching four days of hate from the Republican convention and still standing behind a president who lies his way into a war that tortures and kills innocent people? Then they talk about how their God is about love and compassion.

How, if at all, has your religious community alienated you from the community as a result of your mental illness?

I feel that my own religious community (at least the one I used to feel part of) condemns me for it. They seem to be loving in their judgmental belief that it is my bad karma that gives me this and I have no hope of achieving the ultimate goal in this lifetime, unlike them, who will make it themselves and are further along anyway. When first diagnosed, I sought the counseling of one of the senior monks in the organization and he pretty much said that I need to seek professional help (which I was already getting from mental health professionals) and the church could not help me until I sort out my mental problems. Once I got those sorted out, they could then talk to me about my spiritual issues.

On the other hand Bramachari Lee, a less senior monk, has checked up on me every couple of months. Knowing my spiritual crisis, he has been very supportive without bringing the spiritual conflict into his acceptance of me. He has shown what true spiritual compassion is.

How could your religious community have done a better job in dealing with your mental illness?

I can't think of anything they could do.

Please include any additional comments about your mental illness and your path toward religious identity below.

No other comments. **This is the end of the email questionnaire.**

I sent a copy to my spiritual mentor (Bramachari Lee, who I mentioned in the answers in the questionnaire) and he showed up at my doorstep the next day. He knows me better than anyone. He knew right away that I was in serious trouble and was reaching out for help. He helped me out that day more than any moment in my life.

I still have not sorted it out fully. I must accept that I am agnostic at this point in my life. I know it seems like I am some kind of anti-religion bigot, but I am actually only anti-fundamentalist, and am trying to reconcile it with my lifelong desire for God that is currently clouded by my 'dark night of the soul'.

I know from direct personal experience that good spiritual habits are central to the way out of the 'dark night of the soul'. From study, it seems that the dark night is common to all spiritual seekers, and is possibly a stage close to becoming the saint I have always wanted to be. Jesus had his dark night during the forty days in the desert. It is a time of doubt and confusion that must be faced. I am facing it now.

The Bipolar Advantage may be that we somehow have the ability to perceive beyond our 'shared reality' because we don't have the filters that keep us from hallucinating and experiencing delusions. Maybe 'shared reality' is the real delusion (the Hindus call it Maya) that keeps us from God , and we bipolars have an easier time of breaking the grip of reality to see beyond it. Or, perhaps the

Bipolar Advantage is that we suffer so much that we have a great need to get beyond the suffering and look for the meaning in life. In any case, it seems that in spite of those who see mental illness as a punishment from God, many of the mentally ill are listed as great saints from every religious tradition, and we tend to express greater interest in and hostility to religion than those inflicted with a so-called 'normal' life.

Again, please don't misunderstand that what I often express in this book means that I am anti-Christian or anti-religion. I am trying to show how bipolar effects us very deeply emotionally, physically, and spiritually. Although what I share throughout the book about attitudes towards religion and God were true at the time, they no longer are and I am struggling very hard to reconcile my previous deep faith with the turmoil that came with facing bipolar for the first time in my life. My intent is to show how extreme our thoughts can become, not to attack anything but the fanaticism and fundamentalism that is currently running rampant in all faiths and is counter to the deeper truths of every religion in the world.

Since my diagnosis, the desire to act out in inappropriate ways has diminished a great deal, and my bad habits have been dropping away because they no longer have meaning. At the same time, my desire to experience God directly like I used to is getting so strong I can hardly hold it off any more. I want to pursue the spiritual life with an intensity I have never felt before, and I sincerely want to make a positive difference in the world.

Being diagnosed as bipolar is the best thing that ever happened to me. It has helped me see exactly what I have to overcome to become the person I want to be, and has given me enough pain that I have no other choice but to pursue it with everything I have.

Let's Talk About Sex

Remember in the movie 'The Hours' when Virginia Woolf told her niece that she was going to kill off one of the characters of her book and everyone ran out as fast as they could? What do you mean you never saw it? It is a 'must see' in bipolar movies. Well, I am about to start talking about sex, so run to the fireplace right away and burn this book.

Why is everybody so screwed up about sex that we can't even have an honest and frank discussion about it? I remember in one of my support group meetings a pretty young woman about 30 years old started talking about how she was having trouble with her sexual desires being in conflict with her morals. I was getting ready for her to entertain us with her escapades and she said, "I've been dating this nice man for a couple of months now and I am afraid I might kiss him on the next date." I just lost it. I blurted out, "maybe you need to change your morals to match your desires." She was so offended I thought she would never come back, but she did, and it made me realize how confused people are about sex. Thirty years old, five dates, a kiss is a sin, I guess even I can still be shocked about sex!

I really don't want to offend anyone, but every top ten list I have ever seen about bipolar traits is that we are sexually promiscuous. I thought I knew what that meant, but five dates and no kiss? Isn't that a sin of omission or something? Forget her. Let's talk about the truth.

Bipolar people have a tendency to be not only promiscuous (however you define it), but also to engage in sexual behavior that is dangerous. The danger to bipolar people comes in two flavors, health and social acceptance. We need to honestly assess those dangers if we are to turn sex into a bipolar advantage instead of a risk.

Health Issues

When I was younger I really didn't think I had that much more sex than anyone else. I know now that I did, but back then I thought everybody experimented with sex. My official philosophy was "If I can think of it I should try it, and if I don't like it, I should try it again just in case I was prejudiced against it the first time." I'll leave it up to you to figure out what that means, but I assume you know from the brainstorming topic that I can think of a lot of things!

I heard about disease, but I was invincible. Sound familiar? What delusions do you have that you think you are above the risks? I remember going to the hospital clinic one afternoon because it burned every time I urinated and my penis was dripping some white pus. I thought it was all so funny. The nurse did her examination and left the room. When she came back she was carrying a stack of cards and handed me one. She said "You have 'the clap' (gonorrhea) and you will need some penicillin to clear it up. Don't worry everything will be alright, but you should share this card with your last partner." I just laughed and told her she better give me the whole stack and that was just for last night!

Needless to say I was practicing very dangerous behavior from both a health and social standpoint. I thought "if you don't have sex with me on the first date then what is the point of a second one?" Found three long-term relationships that way and the recent one is going on fifteen years, so go ahead and judge me if you want.

I was actually celibate for a few years(!), including the two years I was in the monastery and the year after. About a year after I had left the monastery I was picked up by a college girl who took me home and gave me a bath before seducing me. While bathing she told me about her promiscuous behavior and about how she learned to be safe. She told me about AIDS, which had become known while I was out of touch with the world (We didn't even read the news in the monastery). My cavalier attitude was a thing of the past. You don't just get the clap or some other harmless disease, you DIE if you're not careful. It was the perfect start to my second life as a sex freak. I had to leave a lot out, but it was easy to find things that would still fulfill my needs without risking my life.

I learned a lot that night, and had a good time to boot! I learned to get tested on a regular basis to make sure I not only find out about HIV for my own good, but to insure that I am not the one who passes death on to someone else. I learned to always use a condom if I am going to do 'at risk' behavior, and to prefer to do things that are considered safe by the medical community. I also learned that the religious right was making shit up to scare people into their warped view of reality that says sex is bad for any reason. I learned that the same clinics that the religious right was blowing up were the only places giving real advice to try to save your life. Most importantly, I learned that I could live according to my morals and still be safe by modifying my behavior to accommodate the risks involved.

We don't need to go into specifics here, but unless you are willing to honestly and openly discuss your behaviors with someone who can help you assess the risks of disease, you are doing an immoral act in anyone's book. Seek out a professional that counsels people in this arena. I assure you that you will not shock her or tell her anything she has not already heard a thousand times.

If you think you have done something no one else has done before, go to sexaholics anonymous and tell your story. Or just sit down and listen to their stories. I'm sure you will get my point that the counselor has heard it all. Just make sure you don't buy into the idea that sex is such a horrible thing. The people who believe that are more messed up than we are.

Morals

Morals is such a touchy issue. There are essentially two types of morals, those that guide your life and those that people try to impose on everyone else. Sex is always held up as the example, instead of the things that really matter like wars, killing, and corporate greed. Let's talk about the second type of morals first, since that is the crux of the problem.

How can anyone push their morals on someone else? Because they know what is right? Because they are following the dictates of the one real God and everyone else is wrong? Because they don't live up to their own rules so they make themselves feel better by cramming their rules down everyone else's throat? Whatever the reason, it is the greatest sin in the world. It is alright to live by YOUR own rules but that does not obligate ME to live up to them. Sure, society will fall apart if people go around shooting each other, but there are laws for that.

Sure I have morals. Everybody does. I just don't believe in forcing my views on anyone. I don't believe in forcing myself on anyone. I don't believe in hurting anyone (even if I have failed on that one more times than I can count). I don't believe in torture. I don't believe in meddling in other people's business. I don't believe killing anyone for any reason can be justified. I don't believe that anyone has a better line on God than I do. I don't believe anyone has a right to interpret God for me. I find all of those things to be deplorable and the worst sins against humanity because of all the pain and suffering they cause.

I DO believe in accepting people for who they are and being respectful of their beliefs while maintaining my right to believe differently. I do believe in trying to treat people in a way that they will feel better about themselves. I do believe in helping to create more love in the world. I do believe that every person has a right to do what they want, as long as it is not harmful to others. I do believe that what I do with a willing adult is NONE OF YOUR BUSINESS.

You need to come up with your own moral beliefs. You can use introspection to find out how you truly feel and what outside influences you either accept or choose not to. Once you have a basic set of morals you can add and subtract from them for the rest of your life. You can try your best to live up to them while accepting your failures. Once you start living by your own set of morals, you will find that life works much better for you.

I meant it when I told the woman she needed to change her morals to fit her desires. I am not advocating for anyone to decide that killing is OK. I am talking about sex. Nobody has the right to impose their sex standards on anyone else. I feel it is equally bad for the religious right to impose their uptight rigidity and misguided misinformation about sexual health on the youth. I think they are doing huge damage imposing their morals on innocent youth who do not have the strength to think for themselves yet. Children are not developed enough to handle their own stuff much less the stuff imposed on them by an adult. Besides, all the crap the right lays on the youth doesn't even work. I know what your kids don't tell you because they don't even trust you enough to have an open conversation with you. I guess you'll have to read the relationships chapter to learn how to find out for yourself.

Drugs

Why do we take drugs?

Do you remember the first time you took drugs? Who were you with? What did you take? Why did you take them? Wrong. You were very young. You were with your mother. You took aspirin. You had a fever.

Drugs are such a central part of our society that we don't even recognize how they influence us. Ever since we were young we have been told by our parents, our doctors, our friends, and our government, that drugs are the key to life. No matter what the condition; there is a drug for it.

My sister Laura started shooting up at three days old. She was born with congenital adrenal hyperplasia, a rare disease that affected her adrenal glands. The innovative treatment that worked for her was using hydrocortisone (the steroids that football players take) as a way to keep her alive. She also suffers from so many side effects it sometimes seems like it was not worth it. Of course, for her the choice was literally between life and death.

We all have taken drugs our whole lives. Not all of us have done illegal drugs, but it is safe to bet that most bipolars have. Sex and drugs are both top issues in every listing of bipolar traits. Along with Rock and Roll we have three of the biggest 'evils' of mankind as central traits. Are we lucky, or what?

What is good about drugs?

My sister Laura would not be alive without drugs. Bipolar people in particular owe much of their success in dealing with our symptoms to the effectiveness of drugs in treating our condition. Research into various pharmacological agents has produced cures that can truly be called miraculous. Mankind has seen tremendous benefits for so many years that it is reasonable to claim that drugs are some of the best things man has ever discovered or created.

At this point in medical history it seems that drugs are the greatest cure for most conditions, especially mental health issues. In the future, drugs may take a back seat to some new therapy, but for now the pharmacy is the central weapons locker for the war on mental illness. Combined with therapy, drugs are a requirement in any realistic treatment of bipolar. The American Psychiatric Association considers it malpractice if a doctor does not prescribe drugs for those diagnosed as bipolar.

For many people, drugs can make the difference between a life of hell and a productive life that approaches 'normalcy' in every way. It is not my intention in this book to go into specifics about drugs and which ones to take. That is why we have psychiatrists. The best and ONLY source for advice on drugs should be your doctor. In our support groups we often share our personal experiences including our frustrations with drugs, but even then, we all agree that it is best to consult your doctor before making any changes to your drug regimen.

There is no doubt that drugs can be a life saving answer to our problems. Properly supervised by your doctor, drugs can create a miracle in your body and mind. It can make such a powerful difference to be on the correct drug regimen that it is understandable why many people feel that drugs are the cure. In fact, many believe that there is no other work necessary once you find the right doctor to prescribe the right drugs for you. Unfortunately, that leads them right into the down side of drugs.

What is bad about drugs?

I talked about how drugs have kept my sister alive. Well, they also made her life a hell that often did not seem worth living. You've no doubt heard about the side-effects that football players get from steroids. How would you like to have been taking them all of your life? By the time Laura was thirty she had metal hips, metal shoulders, addictions to pain killers, nerve damage, hallucinations, and more. Whenever I think my life is hard, I think about Laura and the fact that she has kept a positive attitude with a life nobody else could even bear. To think that drugs are some kind of miracle that has only good effects is the worst delusion imaginable.

Every drug has what is called a 'therapeutic ratio.' This is the difference between the amount that has the desired effect and the amount that will kill you. A commonly used over-the-counter product like aspirin has a therapeutic ratio of around 1:20. Two aspirins are the recommended dose for adult patients. Twenty times this dose, forty aspirins, may cause a lethal reaction in some patients, and will almost certainly cause gross injury to the digestive system, including extensive internal bleeding[1]. Lithium, on the other hand, is much more dangerous. For me, 1500 milligrams is the suggested dose and 2500 milligrams will kill me. 1500 takes away most of my symptoms, but it is hard to tell since I spend the day huddled over the toilet puking.

The point is, drugs may have benefits, but not without side-effects, including death. And the side-effects aren't limited to the physical. There are many psychological side-effects to drugs that need to be considered. Most importantly, drugs make people think that it is the drug that produces the effect and there is no need to do anything else. For that reason alone, it is very critical that you look at drugs with caution. To think drugs are some kind of panacea that have nothing but good to offer is the worst kind of foolishness.

Drugs your doctor prescribes

The drugs your doctor prescribes are an important part of the path to turning bipolar into an advantage. Although I believe it may be possible to do it without drugs, the American Psychiatric Association does not agree. You might note that I take lithium and do not see a time when I will not be on some medication for my condition, although one can always hope.

The American Psychiatric Association says drugs need to be combined with therapy to be effective, so obviously they agree that drugs are not the only answer. As I

---

1 www.alcp.org.nz/info/myths.htm

mentioned in the section on what is bad about drugs, don't think you only need to find a doctor who gives you the right medicine and you are cured. Just as you cannot treat your condition without drugs, you must use therapy and the steps outlined in this book if you are to successfully turn bipolar into an advantage for you.

Your doctor is the best source for medication, but you need to take an active role. Ask questions and learn as much as you can about the different drugs and how they work. Get feedback from fellow patients so you can learn how each drug acts differently in each individual. Work with your doctor to find the best dosage for you. Make sure you are giving your doctor honest and accurate information about what is really going on, so she can help you to determine the right mix of drugs and the right dosage of each.

One area I strongly believe in is sticking to a particular drug long enough to know if it is right for you. I see so many bipolars who constantly switch from one drug to the next without giving any of them a proper trial. The doctor is complicit in this if she lets you, but many of them are willing to let you try different drugs on the hope that you will stick to the one you had a role in selecting. As much as I think you should take an active partnership role with your doctor, she needs to be the boss when it comes to choosing drugs and making sure you give each choice a proper trial.

I am very positive about micro-adjustments to the dosage of drugs. Just because the book says 1500 milligrams is the right dose, it is not necessarily the right dose for you. You need to work with your doctor to adjust the dose to what produces the effect you want. I do not want to be drugged into a zombie state no matter how much those around me prefer it. I want to find a range that makes me feel alive and intelligent. 1500 milligrams of lithium makes me so dull that life is not worth living. With my doctor, I have very slowly lowered my dosage to the point where I just started to lose control and then raised it back to where it cuts out the bad highs as well as the horrible lows. I still have a range of emotions that is greater than non-bipolars, and it works for me. A very slight increase and I feel too sluggish and a very slight decrease and I am too agitated. Find a doctor willing to work with you on this and you will be amazed what you can accomplish together.

You should not be afraid of drugs if you work with your doctor. The pharmaceutical industry has made incredible advancements in drug therapies and they have paid off in a major way for those of us who are trying to control our condition. Don't fall into the trap that makes you think drugs are the only answer and you can use drugs as a critical component in your effort to turn bipolar into an advantage for you.

Self-Medication

And you thought SEX was bad. Self medication is the part of bipolar that causes the most trouble for all of us. More lives are ruined from self medication than from any other cause. Bipolar people have a major DISADVANTAGE here; we destroy our lives and those around us in an ignorant attempt to use drugs to hide our condition. We do it so well that people don't even realize that we are different from an ordinary drunken asshole. The sad truth is we fool everyone so well that they don't understand what we are up against, and they judge us harshly when they should be more understanding of our condition.

My father used alcohol for self medication. Turns out he was diagnosed bipolar when he was in his mid-fifties and had been self medicating his condition his whole life.

I did a lot of self medicating too. Smoked pot like there was no tomorrow. Psychedelics were my favorite, but I tried everything I could find. I took each trial to the extreme, of course. "If it is worth doing, it is worth overdoing," was my motto. I must say, my choice of drugs made me less belligerent, at least while I was on them. My father taught me to stay away from alcohol, the drug of choice for abusive assholes with or without bipolar. I guess you could say I learned from bipolar way before I even knew about it!

It is unbelievable the things I have seen while working with bipolar people. What a bunch of drug addicts. Talk about fucked up - these people can't tell where the drugs end and the hallucinations begin. Just make a bipolar comfortable enough to admit it and you will hear stories that make your ears bleed. There is no better argument for NOT doing drugs than to listen to a bipolar tell stories of drug abuse. If you can find a drug addict that has worse stories than us you should bring him into the clinic and have him interviewed, he is probably bipolar and doesn't know it yet.

The worst thing about it all is that those around us have no idea. They judge us harshly. They try stupid methods to try to stop our drug abuse. They cause more problems than they can imagine. Why can't they figure it out? We have a serious mental illness that is so out of control we can't help but try to use drugs to alleviate it. We don't do it to rebel from our parents. We don't do it to be cool. We are seriously fucked up and will try anything to hide from the truth. Drugs make us think that our condition is caused by the drugs, and that is somehow easier than facing the fact that we are mentally ill.

I hallucinate just fine without taking LSD. So why did I take it? Maybe I needed a reason that is outside of myself. Taking LSD gave me an excuse. Even when not on it, I can claim it is a flashback when I hallucinate. Sure beats admitting my mind is so out of control I can't even walk down the street without seeing things that are not there. If I can drug my mind into submission by getting so drunk or stoned that I pass out, at least I can feel like I was in charge for a while instead of the bipolar condition. I know it doesn't make any sense. Stop trying to figure it out. We are mentally ill.

It is so sad when a mom or dad drags a child to a support group. The poor kid just sits there while dad tells us what is wrong with his kid. Like somehow dad has a clue. I hate him. He has never done anything and he thinks he speaks for his child. "My son does drugs because he thinks he is cool." "My daughter is just trying to rebel." I try to help, but I usually just hold my tongue hoping that the kid will be shoved in the room all alone and left to fend for himself the next time. Mom and Dad don't have a clue and never will until they learn to accept the child and encourage an open and honest discussion.

It is so great when the kid is dumped alone with us. She is dying to tell us what is really going on. She knows from our conversation that we are not like her parents, her minister, or even her doctor. "We've been there. We can help"[1]. If you had any idea about the drugs your child has tried you would shoot yourself from misplaced guilt. You are going about it all wrong and until you figure that out you are only doing more harm than good.

The right way to talk about drugs

Gabriel and Jennifer dragged their daughter Hannah to our support group meeting a couple of years ago. They were not that different from any other family, but the three of them stayed committed long enough to become two great parents and one aware child. Their story is about drugs interwoven with many aspects of the bipolar experience.

It always starts out the same. Mom and Dad go on and on about how their daughter is so messed up and they don't know how they can handle it. It's all about them at that point. The kid always just sits there with the look of 'they don't have a clue.' We never get to hear the kid with the actual illness tell what it is like. And then half of them never come back because we didn't give them some magical phrase that will make everything alright.

Next time only one parent and the kid show up. If it's Dad he flat out says, "I love my little girl," while Mom usually utters, "I don't know how much longer we can stay under the same roof together." Of course the roles are reversed when the kid is a boy. The kid looks genuinely happy to see us because it is fun to see us tell Mom and Dad what can't be said at home. She usually pipes up a little bit and acts like she finally found someone who understands. Still pretty tentative though, mom and dad really don't get

---

1 DBSA motto - www.dbsalliance.org/

it. After two visits half of them drop out and never come back - this condition is way too painful to actually face.

I couldn't help but crack up the time some Dad brought his son on the third visit and just shoved him in the door and walked away. Hannah's parents came together this time and said they were committed to seeing it through. They admitted they didn't know what to do and felt bad that they were not doing a good job. We had an honest and frank discussion about what they all agreed was REALLY going on, while admitting they had a long way to go to making Hannah feel comfortable enough to make them a full partner in the challenge.

We sure heard the scoop from the guy whose father shoved him in earlier. He knew he was helping Hannah to expose her parents to what was going on and he did a command performance. He told us his dad was a fundamentalist idiot who thought his son was still a virgin. He talked about the drug abuse like an old drunk you might meet on the street. And he was 15! Hannah's parents got a priceless lesson and Hannah opened up a lot.

After several very productive weeks, the whole family attended one of our Bipolar In Order Workshops. They really liked the concept of acceptance, and began introspecting as individuals and also as a group. They started learning how to let Hannah share her real life with them and how to support her no matter how hard it was to do. The rest of us got an amazing lesson, and every one of us made contributions to help them.

We all felt strongly about Hannah. I had a special relationship with her because we shared the worst trait of all, we both tear people apart verbally when we go into a rage. All of us could see ourselves in Hannah, and she was only 15. It was clear to everyone in the support group that her life was a total hell and she had a chance that we never had: to do something about it at an early age. Hannah could keep up with the best of us in drugs, sex, and craziness in general. No, we didn't do them with her. We only shared our stories and our feedback.

Hannah did something none of us had done, even if we had heard or thought of it before. She cut herself. She took razor blades to her forearms, not to bleed to death, just enough to feel intense pain. The pain put her in the moment, but there was way more to it than that. She was purposely mutilating herself because she was beautiful on the outside (she truly was) and so ugly on the inside. It produced a drug-like high. She did it to increase the high from other drugs. She did it because she was bored and didn't have anything else to do. She did it because she would rather be dead than endure another day of the hell that was her life.

This was no picnic for Mom and Dad, either. They broke up, got back together, broke up again, took anti-depressants, drank heavily, fought with each other, fought with Hannah, wanted to kill themselves, wanted to kill each other, and showed the deepest love and commitment I have ever seen. They decided after the workshop that Hannah should have the chance to come all by herself to the support group. It became Hannah's choice to come alone or bring one or both of them. Gabriel and Jennifer don't believe it, but in the process they became the best parents on the planet. We all wish we had parents like Hannah's.

Hannah still has a lot of things she hides from her parents, some of which she hides from us as well. She has never shown us what she did to herself with the razor blades. None of us have ever totally opened up, so Hannah is doing as well as any of us. She did open up a lot with us when alone, and over the past few years she has grown incredibly. She admits it when she does something wrong. She takes responsibility for her actions. She tries as hard as she can to improve, while trying just as hard to accept the way she is now.

A woman who was the most delusional person I ever met started coming to the support group. (She hated every song on the radio because she wrote them all and they broke into her house and stole them off her computer. Did I mention they were 60's songs and they didn't even have computers way back then?) She started out giving us dirty looks when we talked about sex or drugs, but just like a good fundamentalist, she graduated to rude comments when she got away with the dirty looks. Pretty soon she was saying God would torture us for eternity if we kept talking about sex or drugs. We asked her to quit coming because she was scaring everyone away, but you know how fundamentalists are. They have some kind of mission to cram their bullshit down everyone's throat.

It all came to a head when the fundamentalist threw out three people before I got there because they didn't fit her profile of a 'good christian' and she started threatening to call the police if we continued to talk about drugs. Right then a new 15 year old boy started telling us about how he did LSD for 30 days straight and his dad, who had just pushed him in the room didn't even know it. He decided on the 31st day that he was going to take four hits, add some Ketamine (a horse tranquilizer popular with the out-of-body experience fans), throw in some Methamphetamine, and some Ritalin for good measure. Now there's a kid who knows how to mix his drugs! He got so fucked up he hung himself by the neck from the rafters and masturbated, trying to time his orgasm for when he died from the choking.

The fundamentalist lost it! Hannah calmly rolled up her sleeves and for the first time, we all saw her arms. She held out her arms, and no matter how many times I heard about it, it didn't dawn on me until that moment what she had actually done to herself. Her arms were so crisscrossed with scars from the razor blades you could not find a place to do it again. She had said before that she had cut her whole body, so I assume it all looks like that.

Mind you, Hannah is now 16 years old. With her arms displayed on the table, she turns to the boy and says, "I have been working on this for a couple of years now and I know exactly how you feel." The fundamentalist bitch dropped her jaw somewhere between "I'm calling the police" and "you will all rot in hell for this." Fortunately for us, she stopped preaching long enough for Hannah to finish.

Hannah said, "I tried all those drugs, cut my body to pieces, tortured everybody around me, and tried to kill myself more times than I can count. These people helped me to face myself and my life is worth living now. I haven't cut myself in three months, no more drugs except the ones my doctor gives me for five months now, and I've made great strides in every part of my illness. If you tell these people what is really going on, they will help you more than you can imagine."

I turned to the fundamentalist and said, "That is why we talk about drugs." It was her complete lack of understanding and willingness to see reality that amazed all of us. She immediately replied "Well, I am calling the police right now," and we all said "fuck you" and walked out. I called Hannah a week later and told her I couldn't take the fundamentalist bitch any more. She said nobody was going back. Hannah said she really needs our support, but cannot take any more of the fundamentalist bullshit. She would have to make it on her own from now on.

Now you know why I hate fundamentalists. It has nothing to do with religion, God, Jesus, or anything. It is about the intolerance and hatred that is constantly spewing from their mouths.

Parents - don't freak out. Your kid is fine. I told you about the worst cases. I'm sure your kid is much better than that. But don't take my word for it. Read the chapter on relationships and find out for yourself what your child is really up to.

Relationships

If you don't have ruined relationships in your past, you better have your diagnosis checked; you are probably not bipolar. With delusions of grandeur, paranoia, arrogance, mood swings, rages, and more, is it any wonder why we can't keep relationships? It seems that relationships are the first casualty of Bipolar Disorder.

It is not only possible, but probable, that as you put Bipolar In Order will you find that building relationships is actually one of the Bipolar Advantages. We have the opportunity and ability to create relationships on a much deeper and intimate level than you ever dreamed possible. We have an intimate understanding of feelings and direct experience of how relationships can go wrong.

There are two critical components to every relationship: communication and commitment. Although we usually try to blame the other party for the failings shared by both sides, our Bipolar Advantage can help us to become the ones that bring out the best in all of our relationships. By learning how to become the best listeners and give the supportive responses the other party is looking for, as well as express what we are looking for in a relationship, we can use our intimate understandings to create open and supportive relationships. Through understanding and awareness we can learn to make the worst part of bipolar into truly the greatest Bipolar Advantage of all.

There are so many areas where our techniques can improve relationships. Our doctor/patient relationship is the best place to start if we are to become the partners we need to be in helping put Bipolar In Order. Of course, our spouse and family relationships should and can be our greatest refuge and source of support. If we are going to function in society, we need to learn how to get along with co-workers because this is an area that can bring out the worst in us. We often feel ill at ease with the general public, mostly from our own misperceptions and fears. This can become another of the Bipolar Advantages once we learn the dynamics of communication. Another important area for us is support groups, both formal and informal. By understanding how relationships work we will learn how to identify our needs, as well as the needs of others, so we can be open and supporting in all of our relationships. Relationships have an impact on every part of our lives.

Our relationship with others so often defines for us how we are handling bipolar and whether it is 'In Order' or 'In Disorder'. Relationships seem like the hardest part of bipolar, but with tools and understanding along with a commitment to accept where we are while striving to be better, they can truly be the biggest Bipolar Advantage of all.

How relationships get off on the wrong foot

What we all do is tell something about ourselves that should elicit a response, then wait to see how well we are accepted. If that goes well we tell something a little more sensitive. If that goes OK, we start to feel like that topic at least is one we can discuss with acceptance with that person or group. If not, we check off that topic as one never to bring up again. It is sad that we have to keep a mental list of topics that can and cannot be brought up.

We find some people who are so limited in acceptable topics that we feel uncomfortable with them. Try talking to my fundamentalist relative and you will know what I mean. She actually thinks that bipolar is God's punishment for not accepting Jesus as my personal savior. Some relationships just aren't worth having.

Unfortunately, we rarely find someone with whom we feel comfortable discussing our deepest feelings and feel we have a real "connection" with. We can be that person for others though, because we feel so deeply that we can empathize. We just have to learn how to communicate with others in a way that makes them feel secure in sharing with us, as well as secure in hearing our side. This is another 'Bipolar Advantage' that we can develop on the road to putting 'Bipolar In Order'.

Acceptance

I have taken some risks in telling you things about myself in this book. Do you accept me the way I am? Are you comfortable with me telling you more intimate details about my life?

Just as with your own bipolar condition, you need to come to an acceptance of others before you have a chance at establishing a relationship that works. Only this time you must accept the person for who he is without trying to change him. You have to surrender to that person's right to be who he really is. The first topic in counseling before marriage is often, "your spouse is not going to change, so don't think that you are going to change him after you get married." Acceptance of others means accepting who they are, not who you want them to be.

Commitment

Show me a relationship that has not had problems and it will be either very young or very superficial. All relationships have troubles if there is any depth to them. Sure, you have had a relationship with the person at the grocery store for years, but does she know what a jerk you can be? And of course a new relationship is perfect since you don't know anything about each other yet.

Sooner or later relationships hit a rough spot. Mine sure have. It is how you work through the tough times that defines the relationship. Do you just quit? Do you just stop talking about the topic that you disagree on? Do you seek counseling? Do you have open and honest conversations and work it out? Do you yell and scream until your partner dumps you? Working through the rough spots is what relationships are all about.

Ellen and I have sure had our differences. Had? Still do. With my bipolar condition and my lifestyle, what do you expect? Throw in Ellen's stuff, and it sometimes seems like a miracle we have made it this far. After 15 years together we still play the same stupid games. Thankfully, not nearly as often.

Our favorite game was "I'm going back to the monastery" and "I'm moving back to France." Ellen taught art at the National Art Academy in Aix en Provence, France. I lived in a monastery. We both lived in our respective 'there' at the same time and met each other a year after we came back to the 'real' world. Threatening to go back there was our favorite argument. Right. Go back to the place you left. If it worked while we were there, we would still be there.

Finally one day we both just started laughing. Ellen said she was going back to France and I joked "Who are we fooling, we're stuck together. We are more miserable apart than we are together." We both cracked up and started holding each other. We resolved to never play that game again. Of course we failed, but we hardly ever play that game or any others except the game of love. Not just the sex kind; real love, committed to each other and the relationship between us.

I decided to start saying "Love is commitment, not the feelings of happiness that you share some of the time." Do you think you don't love your partner when you are so mad that you want her dead? If you didn't love her you wouldn't put yourself through it. Anybody you didn't love would have been dumped a long time ago.

There are many other parts to love of course, but without commitment love is not strong enough to find the way through the tough times. Commitment is the difference between 'in' a relationship and 'between' relationships.

Commitment is key to success in everything. You can find excuses all day long for why you quit something, but you are asking the wrong question. If you look back at all the successes of your life, you will find commitment right there keeping you from quitting.

Commitment is a great topic for your introspection. Ask yourself, "in what ways am I acting to show my commitment to my relationship?"

Remember acceptance? Accepting yourself and trying to accept your partner will go a long way toward making it so you don't need to test your relationship any more.

Funny ending. After all those arguments about moving back, the two of us bought the property next door to the monastery where I used to live. Been here almost four years and she loves it here. Me? Can't wait another minute to get back to San Francisco.

Communication

You know you do it. You've done it a thousand times. Me too. Why don't we just go ahead and admit it then? Admit what? Admit that sometimes when you are with other people they say things or do things that you do not approve of and you give them that 'look.' You know the 'look'. It's the one that says "I think you're weird" or "I don't know if I can accept that" or just shouts out "I DO NOT APPROVE." Not to mention the comments you make. You weren't trying to make her feel better, were you? You know just the comments that will hurt the most. You sadistic bastard. You do it on purpose.

Why did we take up this most evil sin and worst bad habit ever? It was taught to us. By our parents. By our friends. By our schools. And especially by our churches. And the lessons were perfect. You don't even know you do it and are probably wondering what I am talking about. The lessons were so perfect that we usually don't even notice what we're doing.

I meet you for the first time. During the conversation, I bring up the fact that I am bipolar. You have that 'look' of fear and confusion. You change the subject very soon. You just told me that topic cannot be discussed honestly between us. I start telling you things that I know you will approve of. I start my checklist on your file so next time we meet I will avoid those topics that you don't like. Pretty soon we don't have much to say to each other except "nice weather" and "how was work?"

I keep one of those lists for everybody I meet. All filed away in my subconscious so I never even know it was accessed. I don't really think about it. I just don't bring up certain topics with certain people.

And you have a list, too. Your list for me says don't bring up fundamentalists and don't encourage him about sex. We all have lists. It is how we keep from getting into fights all day long.

So, what if it seems like it's OK to bring up a topic again with someone? Then we do. This time a little more intimate and detailed. Not too far; you are afraid he might turn on you. You tell him about a part of yourself that means something to you and there is great fear of rejection. You are totally relieved that you have found someone who you can open up with. And then you change to a new topic that he really hates and you never see him again.

We want so much to find someone who would understand how it really is for us on even ONE topic. We will take all kinds of abuse from someone who accepts just one of our traits because she is accepting of the one trait you are the most afraid to bring up with others.

Wouldn't it be great if someone had an answer to all of this? I think I have one, but I can't make it happen all by myself. What if we told the other person what response we were looking for? What if we told ourselves what response we were expecting? Well, that might help us to become more aware of what we want, but it won't solve the problem.

What we need to do is dump the 'look' and stop making rude comments ourselves. Start thinking, "what response is she looking for? How can I make her comfortable enough to tell me more? This is going to be interesting if I do it right." And suddenly total strangers are telling you things about themselves that they have never told anyone. Then you are living such an interesting life and hearing true stories from the actual people living them. You can ask anything you want, too. They are dying to tell you. So why would you ever do the 'look' again?

Pretty soon a lot of us are doing this: changing the world one relationship at a time. Showing the world that with acceptance comes love, and everyone can get along if we just have honest and open relationships that are based on love and acceptance.

Next thing you notice is that other people start to treat you that way, too. You've finally found friends who understand you. And they are sometimes the same friends you had before who you thought would never understand.

Creativity

We all know that artists are 'crazy.' Researchers have found a strong link between Bipolar and artists, writers, musicians, and especially poets[1]. There is no doubt that for them the bipolar condition is a major advantage.

But what about those of us who can't draw, sing, dance, or write poetry? Did we miss out on perhaps the biggest Bipolar Advantage of all? I don't think so.

Creativity is the ability to come up with an idea or a vision. The skill to bring that vision to paper with a new artwork is an entirely different matter. We bipolars are gifted in the ability to come up with great ideas. That is why we are better than anyone at brainstorming. Many of us suck at making the vision into a reality. That is what 'normal' people are for!

The creative temperament and the bipolar condition

Can you guess what I am the most gifted at in the creativity department? I have an uncanny ability to come up

1 Kay Jamison, *Touched with Fire*, page 88, Figure 3-3. New York, Free Press Paperbacks, 1994

with the exact phrase with the fewest words that will hurt someone the most. I may have a total lack of common sense, but I sure am creative. I did admit to being an asshole savant. I have met a lot of bipolars who smile and agree that they have the same knack. It is the first bad habit for us to replace (or at least tone down) and shows up on many introspection lists.

If we look within, we can all see that we have the creative temperament, even if it has not been harnessed for good. Just like with everything else bipolar, we need to recognize the trait, accept ourselves, and start finding ways to turn it into an advantage.

So how do we recognize our creative advantage? Start by watching for those moments when we have creative thoughts. Don't worry about whether those thoughts are good or not; just start to notice that we are creative and it is an advantage. Don't worry, either, that we never seem to carry out the great ideas that we have. When creativity becomes our own Bipolar Advantage, we will have figured out how to use it for good AND bring the ideas to fruition.

Try it now. Make a list of ways you have been creative. Just like when you brainstormed about bipolar traits, the list should have both good and bad items. Lets see; great suicide plans, cuttingly snide remarks, change the world ideas, new sex tricks, new substances to abuse, funny puns, great inventions, delusions of grandeur, brilliant insights... the list can go on forever! Face it, you are a creative genius. All you have to do is learn how to control your habits and turn creativity into a Bipolar Advantage.

Harnessing your creative potential

Now that you admit that you are creative, why aren't you a great artist? Maybe painting, working with clay, and singing are not skills that you wanted enough to develop. Maybe you just don't have the talent. You are probably stuck in the thought that making art is the only creative thing you can do. Actually, the most creative thing you can do is come up with creative thoughts. The inability to turn those ideas into reality might be one our worst bipolar disadvantages.

I believe that with enough time and effort anyone can develop the skills necessary to complete their creative idea. Skill is over-rated though. How many people have been recognized as great artists even with minimal skills? So many musicians have terrible voices and minimal guitar skills, yet still are among the greats. Don't under-rate skills either, though. Those with great skills AND creativity are the truly great.

So what is more important than skill? Passion. When you have passion for something you are motivated to put in the hard work that it takes to develop great skills. Passion gives you the desire to keep going when finishing your creation seems impossible. Passion gives you the creativity to solve the inevitable problems you encounter along the way. Passion with bad skills usually beats out skills with no passion. Creativity, passion, and skills are the secret to greatness in every field, be it for music, art, or running a popsicle cart.

What are you passionate about? Might be a great introspection question to add to your list. Try brainstorming a list of things you are passionate about. I guess I have to admit that I am passionate about introspection, brainstorming, and sex! I was the Michelangelo of porn - creative, passionate, and skilled; the perfect combination to turn any activity into an art form. Doesn't hurt to be delusional either. 'Manic Depression has given me the ability to do great things in my life, or at least the delusion to think they were!'

You say that some people don't approve of your passion? Your parents wanted you to be a doctor and you wanted to be a painter? People think it's awful that you admit who you really are? Time to tap into another Bipolar Advantage. So they think you are 'crazy?' Take advantage of it and do something 'crazy.' Follow your passion and do what you want to do. If they want a doctor in the family so bad they can pursue it themselves. The 'crazy' ones never turn out the way their parents expected. If we follow our passion we turn out better than even WE expected.

"But I never follow through" you say. Me neither. That is why they invented 'normal' people. When you read the stories of great bipolar people, many of them were what you call 'idea people.' We 'idea people' need to associate with 'normal' people so that they can finish our great plans. They need us just as bad as we need them. More often than not, an 'idea person' without someone to help make it happen fails to finish the project. Just as often the 'normal person' leads a life of mediocrity due to lack of good ideas.

When you figure out how to control the bad habits that are so unattractive to others, you will find that your creativity and passion is VERY attractive to everyone. Don't underestimate your ability to attract people to help in your projects. Everyone is attracted to creativity. How many times has someone found the creative side of you attractive, but was turned off by some of your bad habits? Winners are those who are more attractive with their creativity than repulsive by their bad behavior. You need look no further than great corporate leaders to know what I mean.

My Creativity

While contemplating what to write about my own creativity, it dawned on me that cataloging my past creative ventures was the wrong way to go. Although I can think of many creative things to write about (and no doubt make it entertaining), creativity is about creating the future. To that end, I wish to share with you my vision for the future.

Remembering the good things in my past helps me stay positive in the present, but it is mired with the memories of what was not so good. I need to have a positive vision of the future to stay alive - literally. It is only my ability to see a future worth living that keeps me from letting the current hell take my life. I am at one of those points when I cannot tolerate the present any longer and am searching for a future vision that will motivate me to continue the struggle.

Enough of that. On to the future. I really feel like I found my calling. Having given workshops for many years about topics that I liked, but did not feel passionate about, I am very excited about doing educational workshops about bipolar and depression. I want to write books. I want to give presentations. I want to start a podcast channel. Most of all, I want to move home to San Francisco Bay and drive my boat. Now there is a future worth living! I think I said it before, but it is worth repeating. Bipolar has given me my first career that has REAL meaning to me. It is the only thing I want to do.

Workshops are where I really shine. I love giving the Bipolar In Order workshop and it has been getting very positive feedback from people who have been leaders in the local bipolar support community for years. I am hoping to find a sponsor who will fund the project so that people can attend for free while I still manage to have a reasonable income. I also look forward to starting an advanced workshop that goes much deeper into the topics covered in the first workshop along with new material. Another advantage of an advanced workshop is that we can actually accomplish the changes instead of just talking about them. I really look forward to creating the advanced workshop.

The book is almost complete. I am writing this chapter after all of the edits have been completed on the rest of the book. Writing it was a great experience for me. It helped me to explore the creativity of writing and I really like it. I know I have at least one more book in me, maybe more. I hope to start a second book soon with personal stories that others share with me about the REALITY of their condition. I am looking for people that are interested in sharing their stories now. If you are interested, please contact me through the website - www.bipolaradvantage.com.

I love giving presentations. I have one scheduled for next month and plan to schedule many more once the book is officially out. Most people meticulously work out the details of the presentation for fear of blowing it by being unprepared. I love to have a general outline and, as they say, wing it. Live audiences do something for me and the creativity of it is such a thrill. If you would like a presentation or know someone who might, please let me know.

The idea for a podcast channel came as a result of looking for ways to market the book. There are 16,800,000 web pages about bipolar on Google and exactly zero podcasts about bipolar - until today. What a creative way to bring attention to the book and workshop! Thinking about it and talking with Ellen turned podcasts into the best creative idea this week. I am really into this and hope to accomplish at least some of the ideas.

What started out as a way to market my book and workshops quickly evolved into a much grander vision. My mind is on fire with the idea and I have done massive research into publishing, recording, marketing, etc. all in the last few days. As a matter of fact, I had no idea what to write about creativity until I realized that I was in the most exciting part of the process. I will have the first podcast up this week and hope to have many 'shows' in the works soon.

Ideas for the show run the gamut from boring interviews with doctors to recordings of actual manic rages and people in the depths of depression. I want to record actual support groups so people who have never been to them can get a feel for what goes on. I want to interview people who have written books, famous people who are bipolar, crazies on the streets, and anyone who will sign a waiver releasing me to podcast the recording.

I want to read chapters from my book and riff off of the reading with thoughts and insights that are not in print, much like the director of a movie has a commentary on the DVD. I hope to do the same with other authors.

Most of all I want it to be edgy and REAL. I want people who listen to the podcasts to get a real taste of what it is like to be bipolar or what it is like to be someone who supports or lives with a bipolar person. Just like this book, I want it to shock people into seeing REALITY.

When I start brainstorming visions of the future, family and friends get nervous or say no to many of the ideas. We end up mad at each other. Maybe they think I am going to do every crazy idea that I think of. I finally figured it out just recently. I NEED to have a vision of the future that keeps me alive today. I don't need to necessarily make all of it happen. It is the creativity of the vision and the hope that it engenders in me that makes me think life is worth living.

The Greatest Bipolar Advantage of all

This is what creativity is all about. Coming up with too many ideas is a good thing. Being able to sift through those ideas and find the ones you are truly passionate about, and spend time developing them is a good thing too. Your future is the pursuit of whatever your passion is. Creativity is the greatest Bipolar Advantage of all.

Putting Bipolar In Order

Making life work the way you want it to

Putting Bipolar In Order is about using all the knowledge and tools at our disposal to take what was given to us and make a good or even great life out of it. That includes finding the positive, developing coping skills, making plans that lead to success, living a scheduled life, and maintaining consistency in our effort to improve.

Just like any journey, we must know where we are starting from, where we are going, and where we are at every moment along the way. Bipolar In Order is about developing awareness of our real selves through study, introspection, and the relationships that help us along the path. It is also about practicing the skills that become the important tools to use to achieve our goals. We may not have chosen to be afflicted with bipolar disorder, but we can certainly choose to make the best of it. The lessons, skills, exercises, and shared learning of the Bipolar In Order Workshop and this book can be the key to changing our lives into one that has other people and ourselves saying that bipolar gives us an advantage. This advantage helps make us better people.

What we need to do is develop an action plan for putting Bipolar In Order. All the learning in the world will do no good without a plan that is both effective and achievable. It is of no use to run a marathon one day and not even jog again for another year. In order to be successful in achieving any goal, you must have a plan that helps you to maintain consistency of effort. A good plan coupled with constant effort is what leads to success.

Putting together a plan for success

The most important thing is not to make too many changes at once. Remember, habits take time to develop, and replacing bad habits is very hard to do. If you try too many changes at once you will make it way too hard to establish new good habits and root out the bad ones. It is best to start out slow. Pick the ONE change you are most attracted to and stick with it until you are sure it has become a solid habit.

Once you get one change working for you it is time to pick up another good habit and choose a bad habit to quit. This is a personal thing for each of us, so there is no best plan for everyone.

The first habit everyone should take up is introspection. Introspection is the foundation for every new habit. Without introspection you will not know if you are getting anywhere because you will not know where you are today. Only by introspecting on a daily basis can you honestly know how you are doing. If you implement only one idea from this book, it should be introspection.

A simple meditation practice may be the next best thing to introspection. Whenever I take up changes after I inevitably fall apart (as any bipolar person will), introspection and meditation are the first things I do for many weeks. Once I get those critical habits under control, I can start working on my exercise routine and start picking away at some of the many bad habits that I have.

Creating a vision for the future

Every business that succeeds has a plan. A sound plan is based on a vision for the future. Having a plan for where you want to be acts as the road map to follow. Introspection helps you know where you are on the map, but without clear goals you still do not know which way to go. Putting together a vision and a plan to make it happen is crucial for success.

First, you need to do several visualizations about how you see yourself in the future. Brainstorming might help you come up with alternatives, but visualization will help you see yourself in much greater detail. At the end of a visualization, picture yourself in a future where you are everything you could ever dream of being.

In your visualization try to see every detail. How do you look? How is your health? Is your diet working for you? How is your relationship with your doctor? What career are you in? Where do you live? Are you happy? You can brainstorm a list of questions, and after the visualizations you can write down the answers. You can keep doing this until you have a pretty good idea of where you would like to be some day if everything worked out perfectly for you.

Breaking the vision down into goals

Once you have a vision for the future it is time to make it happen. Just like when taking a trip in a car, you need to know where you are now (introspection) and your destination. In planning a car trip, you take out a map and plan your route. If it is a long trip (and creating your vision is a life long trip), you also need to plan where you are going to get to every day and where you will sleep. To make our vision into a reality we need to plan and map out the trip, too.

The first step in planning is to decide how long it is going to take to get there. Do you want to do it in ten years? Twenty? Thirty? Having a clear goal and arrival date is crucial if you are going to succeed. Every business has a long term goal and considers it in every decision. Once you have a clear goal and a date to achieve it, you have made a huge step in making it happen.

The next step is to break down the goal into smaller parts. Just like the car trip with overnight stays, you need to reach milestones that will let you know when you are achieving success. If the goal is to be achieved in ten years, where are you going to be in five? Write down all of the details that you can about where you will be in five years. If you are going to get to that point in five years, where do you need to be in two? Write down those goals too. Do the same process for one year, six months, three months, two months, one month, three weeks, two weeks, one week, and tomorrow.

Every successful business in the world has clearly defined goals for ten years as well as tomorrow. If you really want to succeed, you should have goals too. The above process will help you in defining those goals, but you also have to see if they are realistic. Can you really accomplish tomorrow's goals? If you can't, you will never make the first week's goal. You need a plan that is both detailed and ACHIEVABLE. Once you have that plan you are on your way.

Making adjustments as necessary

How did you end up THERE? It's not even on the map. You must have taken a wrong turn somewhere. Don't worry, we all do it. Just like in meditation, our mind likes to wander and take us on side trips. It is perfectly natural.

We just need to make adjustments to our plan periodically. The journey is really not about the destination. It is about the journey. As long as we are trying to improve we are on the right path. Remember acceptance? We try to love and accept ourselves while striving to be better people. The plan is to become a better person. Through acceptance we understand that we are not there yet and that we are going to make a lot of mistakes along the way.

Adjusting the plan is easy. When you find yourself off of the plan, change all of the dates so you can get back on the new schedule. If you need to, change your whole plan. Businesses do it all the time. Life never works out the way you plan. You need to be flexible and go with the flow. Flexibility had been mentioned in every Bipolar In Order Workshop as one of our advantages. Sometimes the one thing we need to remember is to be flexible with ourselves.

Now just take what you've learned and go out there and do it. Use your Bipolar Advantage!

I Need Your Help

Ellen says I should call this chapter "Shameless Plug." Actually, one of the many Bipolar Advantages is that after all of the outrageous and embarrassing things we have done, it is easy to ask for help :-) I know that I need all the help I can get and I am not ashamed to admit it.

There are so many ways you can help. Start by contacting me and giving your encouragement. You can send an email via the website www.bipolaradvantage.com if you like. You can also use the website to send me any ideas or suggestions you may have.

It would be great if you can help me get the word out.

The Bipolar Advantage:

- Link to www.bipolaradvantage.com and www.bipolarinorder.org from your website.

- Ask your local bookstore to carry the book, The Bipolar Advantage by Tom Wootton.

- Write a review of the book and submit it to local papers, magazines, websites (www.amazon.com, www.bn.com), etc.

- Tell your doctor about the Bipolar Advantage book and Bipolar In Order workshop.

- Post messages in chat rooms, newsgroups, etc.

- Tell your local DBSA or NAMI support groups.

- Send me referrals, especially corporate officers, pharmaceutical reps, famous bipolars, or anyone else you think might be influential and able to help.

The Bipolar in Order Workshops:

- First of all, take one yourself!

- Arrange to host the workshop in your town.

- Write a review of the workshop and submit it to local papers, magazines, websites, etc.

- Contribute to the scholarship fund so that people who cannot afford it have the chance to attend.

- All donations are tax deductible. Please contact us through www.bipolarinorder.org for more information.

The podcast channel:

- You can subscribe to it.

- Submit ideas and content for future podcasts.

- Tell others about the channel.

- Inform the internet community about the channel.

- Do an interview with me about your book, idea, etc.

Acknowledgments

I had been telling Ellen that I wanted to write a book for several months. I was too depressed to work on it, so I had to wait for the right moment. The inspiration for calling the book 'The Bipolar Advantage' came from Bramachari Lee, who I mentioned in the survey I took. Lee convinced me to look at it as a 'condition' instead of an illness. Once I started to see that bipolar is a 'condition' that has both good and bad components, I started to see that there are actually some advantages along with the pain. Lee's council was instrumental in my learning to deal with my own 'condition' as well as the inspiration for the workshop and this book.

Late May of 2005 we were visited for the second time by Rosemary Graham, a writer from Berkeley, who comes to our retreat to write in what she calls 'The Virginia Woolf Cabin.' Seeing Rosemary for the second visit in a year spurred me on, and with her encouragement, I started writing on June 2nd. By June 8th, I had written over 40,000 words!

My good friend Peter Russell writes many books about consciousness and he remarked that 3,000 words a day is prolific. I was averaging almost 6,000! Without Ellen's encouragement tempered with her careful monitoring of my hypomania, I think I would have slipped into a full blown manic episode. Ellen made sure I kept up my sleep habits while still allowing for creativity to flow. Our agreement was that if I stay up all night one night, I had to take Ativan™ (my favorite sleep aid) and get a good nights sleep the next night. The book would never have been written without the encouragement of Rosemary, Peter, and Ellen. I would have never survived writing it without Ellen's love and support, especially working as monitor of my condition.

For the rest of June I finished the first draft and got myself back to a more normal life. I had to fight the desire to work on the book, but knew that allowing the mania to go too far is dangerous. Ellen's support during that period was invaluable. Ellen's support all the time is invaluable.

My daughter Kate visited during the last week in June. Kate and I spent many hours reading the book together. It was a very special time for me because she learned many things about me that she had never known. We became so much closer from the experience. While reading the book, Kate would have me explain parts that didn't make sense to her, and we rewrote many parts of the book together. Kate is in her last year of undergrad, hoping to go on to medical school. Her editing for grammar was wonderful and I felt great about the book by the time she went back to Boulder.

During the second week of July I stayed at my mother's house and she read the book while I was there. She already knew most of the details. I have always been able to tell her anything. She is my role model for 'relationships' and 'acceptance.' She was very encouraging and helped me to better explain parts of the book. During the same week, my sister Sandy also read over the book and encouraged me to keep working on it. By the time I got home the project had been going for a month and a half and I was deluded enough to think it was ready for publishing.

I mentioned Becca was instrumental on my day of crises when I went to my first support group meeting. I lost touch with her after that, but we started a friendship after she attended one of my Bipolar In Order workshops. After the workshop, Becca became my first true bipolar friendship. When Becca finished looking over my book, she met with me at Panera Bakery for what I thought was an hour lunch. Turned out we were there for about 8 hours! Becca had highlighted so many changes I could not believe it. We made the changes together, often after discussing the options and coming to agreement on how best to phrase things to make the most sense. The book was so much better after Becca's input I was really thinking it was ready for publishing right away.

While Becca was reading over the book, my friend Doug Anthony was doing the same. Doug is a Shaker (Google it) and was very perceptive about the spiritual parts of the book. Doug gave me great feedback that I incorporated right away.

I met Libby Israel while she was leading a support group meeting in La Jolla. I was so impressed with the way she handled the meeting and the fact that she maintains a very stressful, full time position while dealing with bipolar. Libby took a Bipolar In Order workshop at the same time as Becca and both of them encouraged me to keep pursuing my dream. They both talked me into doing another workshop in August and they both attended for a second time.

Ellen and I took a vacation on August 5th and Libby and Jim stayed at our retreat for a week. I left my manuscript for Libby to look over, and by the time we got settled back in, I had the workshop to give on August 12 through the 14th. A week later Libby gave me a set of edits as big as Becca's! I couldn't believe after Ellen, Kate, and Becca made changes that there could possibly be so many, but as I went over them, I agreed with almost every one. Libby really put the book into great shape, and the process so far was only two and a half months!

Ellen and I went over the whole book one more time and made several more changes. By September 20th the book was ready for the printer. Only thing now is the cover. Don Farnsworth is the best graphic genius I ever met. Visit www.magnoliaeditions.com and you will see what I mean. He agreed to help with the cover, so I had to wait until the first week of October to be in San Francisco for a visit with him. His work is never what I had in mind, but always so much better.